Jesus'
Third
Way

VIOLENCE
AND
NONVIOLENCE
IN
SOUTH AFRICA
Jesus' Third Way

Walter Wink

Published in Cooperation with the
Fellowship of Reconciliation

new society publishers

Philadelphia, PA   Santa Cruz, CA

Inquiries about requests to republish all or part of the materials contained herein should be addressed to:

New Society Publishers
4722 Baltimore Avenue
Philadelphia, PA 19143

968

The Scripture quotations contained herein, unless otherwise noted, are from the Revised Standard Version Bible, copyright 1946, 1952, 1971 by the Division of Christian Education of the National Council of the Churches of Christ in the U.S.A. and are used by permission.

ISBN: Hardcover 0-86571-116-X
ISBN: Paperback 0-86571-117-8

Cover design: Mike Holderness
Book design: Barbara Hirshkowitz

This book is printed on partially recycled paper.

New Society Publishers is a project of the New Society Educational Foundation and a collective of the Movement for a New Society. New Society Educational Foundation is a nonprofit, tax-exempt, public foundation. Movement for a New Society is a network of small groups and individuals working for fundamental social change through nonviolent action. To learn more about MNS, write: Movement for a New Society, PO Box 1922, Cambridge, MA 02238. Opinions expressed in this book do not necessarily represent positions of either New Society Educational Foundation or Movement for a New Society.

Contents

About the Author

Dr. Walter Wink is Professor of Biblical Interpretation at Auburn Theological Seminary in New York City. He has also taught at Union Theological Seminary and Hartford Seminary, and has been a visiting professor at Columbia and Drew universities. His published works include *Naming the Powers* and *Unmasking the Powers* (the first two volumes of a trilogy), and *The Bible in Human Transformation*, all from Fortress Press; *Transforming Bible Study* (Abingdon Press); and *John the Baptist in the Gospel Tradition* (Cambridge University Press). He has been active in the American civil rights movement, the anti-Vietnam War struggle, and the campaign for nuclear disarmament. He visited South Africa in March and April, 1986.

A Note to
South African Readers

This book is an attempt to respond to a remark made to me by Beyers Naude, general secretary of the South African Council of Churches, during a forty day visit to South Africa my wife June and I made in March and April, 1986. He said, "In South Africa we have never yet had a thorough discussion of the issue of violence or nonviolence. It is vitally important to form a legitimate theological position regarding that question." Whatever contribution this study may make to that need, it is intended to be, not a solution, but merely a further prod to discussion.

I am painfully aware that I am an outsider, that I speak rather glibly of sufferings I will not be required to bear, that I am a white American not a little complicit in an international system that generally benefits whites at the expense of blacks, and that I do not have an adequate grasp of your situation. I plead only that the arrogance of my intervention into your setting be read as desperate caring for the future of all your peoples. That care was given personal shape by the incomparable hospitality and warm friendship offered us at every turn as we were passed from home to home during our stay. To all who gave up time, beds and food to fuel and sustain our mad dash through your sad and wonderful land, we send our heartfelt gratitude. We pray for your safety, but even more, for your faithfulness in the days ahead.

A fuller and more general discussion of some of the themes presented here will be taken up in *Engaging the Powers*, the third volume of my trilogy, *The Powers*, from Fortress Press.

Nonviolent militant action is crucial in the encounter with principalities and powers, for they are never simply the outer forms of institutions, structures and systems, but also comprise the interiority or withinness of these outer forms—their spirituality. The apartheid phenomenon of South Africa is by no means identical with its present leaders, or the police and military forces, or the bureaucratic apparatus. It is also the ethos of racism; the legitimation of that ethos by a theology which, through the manipulation of Scripture, has deliberately and knowingly advocated injustice; the mentality of the *laager* ("circle the wagons and fight to the last"); and the willingness to resort to inconceivable levels of violence to preserve privilege. Fundamental change in such a setting will require both structural and spiritual transformation. Neither by itself will be enough. "For we are not contending against flesh and blood, but against the principalities, against the powers, against the world rulers of this present darkness, against the spiritual hosts of wickedness in the heavenly places. Therefore take the whole armor of God, that you may be able to withstand in the evil day, and having done all, to stand" (Eph. 6:12–13).

The
Case
Against
Nonviolence
in
South
Africa

Chapter One

There have been some remarkable success stories of nonviolent struggle around the world recently. In the Philippines, a nonviolent revolution led by Corazon Aquino with crucial support from the churches swept the dictator Fernando Marcos from office with a loss of only 121 lives. Central to the effectiveness of that struggle was a background of training in nonviolent direct action provided by the International Fellowship of Reconciliation.

In Poland, Solidarity has irreversibly mobilized popular sentiment against the puppet Communist regime. There, an entire clandestine culture, literature, and spirituality have come to birth outside the authority of official society. This undercuts the oft-repeated claim that what Mohandas Gandhi did in India or Martin Luther King, Jr. did in the American South would never work under a brutal, Soviet-sponsored government.

Nonviolent general strikes have overthrown at least seven Latin American dictators: Carlos Ibáñez del Campo of Chile (1931), Gerardo Machado y Morales of Cuba (1933), Jorge Ubico of Guatemala (1944), Elie Lescot of Haiti (1946), Arnulfo Arias of Panama

(1951), Paul Magliore of Haiti (1956), and Gustavo Rojas Pinilla of Colombia (1957).[1] Gene Sharp has itemized 198 different types of nonviolent actions which are a part of the historical record, yet our history books seldom mention any of them, so preoccupied are they with power politics and wars.[2]

For some reason, however, many people tend to dismiss these instances of nonviolent action as exceptional and of no pertinence to *their* situation, which is, of course, always unique. The question for South Africans seems to be, Will it work here?—or more pertinently perhaps, Why did it not work here? South Africa makes an excellent case study of the question because its struggle is still unfolding, nonviolence is widely considered to have failed, and violence is more and more becoming the first resort by parties on all sides of the conflict. It is, moreover, a nation whose government has exhibited utter disregard for the lives of its opponents and has repeatedly defied both world opinion and the appeals of its few allies to restrain its violence. If nonviolent direct action still can make a direct contribution in South Africa, it should be in principle, at least, a "first resort" in any other conceivable situation of oppression.

We spent forty days in South Africa in March and April, 1986. It is important to date our experience because events are unfolding so fast there that the relevance of this argument needs to be understood within the time frame of our involvement there. Besides interviewing scores of people and visiting homelands and townships, I led four workshops on Jesus' teachings on nonviolence, two with black students and two with predominantly white clergy. In what follows, I will not only be engaged in theological reflection of my own but also reporting on the theological reflections of those with whom we spoke. Since many of my sources, especially blacks, cannot be quoted without possibly endangering them, I have generally not cited them except where their views have been published.

What we found most surprising is that a great many people simply do not know how to name their actual experiences of nonviolence. I put the question to the participants in workshops and to those we interviewed: What do you think of Jesus' teaching about turning the other cheek? Scarcely a single person was prepared to take it at all seriously. The refrain so frequently repeated was, "We tried that for fifty years and it didn't work. Sharpeville in 1960 proved to us that violence is the only way left."

Yet when I pressed these same people to identify the tactics that had proved most effective in the past two years, they produced a remarkably long list of nonviolent actions: labor strikes, slow-downs, sit-downs, stoppages, and stay-aways; bus boycotts, consumer boycotts, and school boycotts; funeral demonstrations; non-cooperation with government-appointed functionaries; non-payment of rent; violation of government bans on peaceful meetings; defiance of segregation orders on beaches and in restaurants, theaters, and hotels; and the shunning of black police and soldiers. This amounts to what is probably the largest grassroots eruption of diverse nonviolent strategies in a single struggle in human history! Yet these students, and many others we interviewed, both black and white, failed to identify these tactics as nonviolent and even bridled at the word.

There are, we learned, good reasons for their reluctance to champion nonviolence. The term itself is negative. It sounds like a not-doing, the putting of all one's energy into avoiding something bad rather than throwing one's total being into doing something good. A new, more positive term is needed. The South African Council of Churches (SACC) has suggested "responsible resistance," as opposed to irresponsible resistance, but that is so ambiguous that it could be stretched to cover even all-out war. I have long sought a better term—an English equivalent of Gandhi's *satyagraha* ("truth-force")—but without success.[3] Therefore I have settled on *Jesus' Third Way*, or simply the Third Way, as a way of denoting the unique quality of creative response Jesus taught and lived.

But the term itself is hardly the cause of objection. "Nonviolence" is identified, especially by South African blacks, with the "white" gospel that taught them that they must always be submissive before the authorities (read "white" authorities). Romans 13:1–7 was interpreted as an absolute injunction to obey the government *whatever it does*. "Turn the other cheek" became a divine command to slaves and servants to accept flogging and blows obsequiously. "Love of enemies" was twisted to render blacks compliant from the very heart, forgiving every injustice with no thought of changing the system. Nonviolence meant, in the context of this perverse inversion of the gospel, passivity. And the oral identity of "pacifism" and "passivism" only made the confusion worse.[4]

Now that these same blacks have said No to apartheid and a resounding No also to the lying gospel that legitimated it, they cannot easily reappropriate the Biblical texts which had been perverted to hold them submissive under violence. And the churches, both white and black, have done very little to help. The English-speaking churches (eighty percent black yet, until recently, led by whites) have for decades been issuing stronger and stronger denunciations of apartheid. But they have been reluctant to translate these lofty sentiments into risky, committed actions. They turned their backs on the Defiance of Laws Campaign of 1952 when nonviolent resistance might have checked apartheid before it could become entrenched. The legacy of white missionary religion with its individualistic, guilt-ridden piety and its dreams of a compensatory afterlife still renders these churches relatively innocuous. When such bodies speak of nonviolence, therefore, it can only be heard as meaning "Don't rock the boat, don't disturb our troubled sleep."

Many whites have developed a sudden new interest in having blacks become nonviolent, and that too must be read as a cynical attempt to avoid the consequences of an unjust system rather than an attempt to address its root causes. Most Christians desire nonviolence, yes; but they are not talking about a nonviolent struggle for justice. They mean simply the absence of conflict. They would like the system to change without having to be involved in changing it. What they mean by nonviolence is as far from nonviolent direct action as a lazy nap in the sun is from a confrontation in which protesters are being clubbed to the ground.

When a church which has not lived out a costly identification with the oppressed offers to mediate between hostile parties, it merely adds to the total impression that it wants to stay above the conflict and not take sides. The church says to the lion and the lamb, Here, let me negotiate a truce, to which the lion replies, Fine, after I finish my lunch.

"Reconciliation" also has been misused. One person we spoke with commented, "The two dirtiest words in black South Africa today are 'nonviolence' and 'reconciliation.'" Reconciliation is necessary, and it must be engaged in at all stages of the struggle. The human quality of the opponent must be continually affirmed. Some kind of trust which can serve as the basis of the new society to come must be established even in the midst of conflict. But when church leaders preach reconciliation without having unequivocally committed themselves to struggle on the side of the oppressed for justice, they are caught straddling a pseudo-neutrality made of nothing but thin air. Neutrality in a situation of oppression always supports the status quo. Reduction of conflict by means of a phony "peace" is not a Christian goal. Justice is the goal, and that may require an *acceleration* of conflict as a necessary stage in forcing those in power to bring about genuine change.

Likewise, blanket denunciations of violence by the churches place the counterviolence of the oppressed on the same level as the violence of the system that has driven the oppressed to such desperation. The *Kairos Document* pointedly asks, "Would it be legitimate to describe both the physical force used by a rapist and the physical force used by a woman trying to resist the rapist as violence?"[5] Are stones thrown by black youth (which so far as I know have not killed a single policeman) really commensurate with buckshot and real bullets fired by police (which in the last two years have killed around a thousand blacks, including infants)?

Most of the South African churches have never, in

fact, been opposed to violence, according to theologian Charles Villa-Vicencio. They have only been opposed to violence in the hands of blacks. The Afrikaner churches have glorified violence in their monuments and histories, and they even celebrate the Battle of Blood River and the Great Trek as divine acts.[6] The British colonialists were no better, with their regimental colors in the chancel decor and stained glass windows.

How then can white Christians condemn black violence and still go on allowing their sons to accept conscription into the armed forces, or appointing army chaplains to legitimate and minister to those involved in suppressing revolt, or paying taxes to support an increasingly militarized and brutal state?[7] Had the churches been unequivocal in providing nonviolent leadership and action all along, they could have perhaps prevailed upon violent black youth to stop the practice of "necklacing" (tires placed over the heads of informers and collaborators, doused with gasoline, and set ablaze). As things stand now, with but few exceptions (Archbishop Desmond Tutu, Reverend Allan Boesak, and others have risked death to save such people), most black clergy would fear for their lives if they denounced such atrocities. The church simply has not paid the price to play moral arbiter in the present crisis.

Most black South Africans, we were told, no longer see a choice between violence and nonviolence. They are simply saying: "We are at war. And in war one chooses tactics that work. If nonviolent tactics are being used, it is merely because they are effective, not because we are committed to a nonviolent philosophy." From this point of view, nonviolent direct actions are regarded merely as one among many strategies for guerrilla warfare and have no intrinsic relationship to principled pacifism.

Finally, some pacifists have been rightly criticized for being more concerned with their own righteousness than with the sufferings of the afflicted. As Dietrich Bonhoeffer argued:

> To maintain one's innocence in a setting such as that of the Third Reich, even to the point of *not* plotting Hitler's death, would be irresponsible action. To refuse to engage oneself in the demands of *necessita*, would be the selfish act of one who cared for his own innocence, who cared for his own guiltlessness, more than he cared for his guilty brothers.[8]

The issue is not, What must I do in order to secure my salvation? but rather, What does God require of me in response to the need of others? It is not, How can I be virtuous? but How can I participate in the struggle of the oppressed for a more just world? Otherwise our nonviolence is premised on self-justifying attempts to establish our own purity in the eyes of God, others, and ourselves, and that is nothing less than a satanic temptation to die with clean hands and a dirty heart.[9]

The case for the use of violence is summed up by Father Buti Tlhagale. In his 1982 Day of Peace message Pope John Paul II declared that Christians have a right and even a duty to protect their existence and freedom by proportionate means against an unjust aggressor. Most blacks see the National (Afrikaner) Party as such an aggressor. It was not elected by blacks but simply imposed itself on them and denied them basic human rights. This government, therefore, has no moral right to govern them, nor to use violence to preserve its intrinsically violent political system. Blacks who resort to violence understand it as an act of self-defense against a system and a people that practices oppression and exploitation. "It is hoped," Father Tlhagale asserts, "that through violence justice will eventually be established."

Limited violence against the regime has undoubtedly attracted the attention of the world community and the local conservative business community, Father Tlhagale continues. The apartheid government only moves when forced to do so, as when the 1976 upheavals finally led to the 1979 labor legislation that for the first time sanctioned genuine unions. No amount of "reform" can make apartheid (or "separate development" or any other separatist scheme) palatable. In the face of the government's intransigence, its cosmetic adjustments, and its trail of broken promises, Tlhagale sees no other recourse but a just or holy war against the state. "That the gospel or the life-history of Christ makes no room for the use of violence to right the wrongs of society remains a massive scandal among the oppressed," despite Jesus' consistent subversion of the religious and political order of his day.[10] In short, Jesus' rejection of the Zealot option raises fundamental questions about the validity of the gospel itself, and more and more blacks are turning to Marxism for answers.

Jesus' Third Way

Chapter Two

Many of those who have committed their lives to ending apartheid simply dismiss Jesus' teachings about nonviolence out of hand as impractical idealism. And with good reason. "Turn the other cheek" suggests the passive, Christian doormat quality that has made so many Christians cowardly and complicit in the face of injustice. "Resist not evil" seems to break the back of all opposition to evil and to counsel submission. "Going the second mile" has become a platitude meaning nothing more than "extend yourself," and rather than fostering structural change, encourages collaboration with the oppressor.

Jesus obviously never behaved in any of these ways. Whatever the source of the misunderstanding, it is clearly neither in Jesus nor his teaching, which, when given a fair hearing in its original social context, is arguably one of the most revolutionary political statements ever uttered:

> You have heard that it was said, "An eye for an eye and a tooth for a tooth." But I say to you, Do not resist one who is evil. But if anyone strikes you on the right cheek, turn to him the other also; and if anyone would

sue you and take your coat, let him have your cloak
as well; and if any one forces you to go one mile, go
with him two miles (Matt. 5:38–41, Revised Standard
Version).

When the court translators working in the hire of King
James chose to translate *antistēnai* as "*Resist* not
evil," they were doing something more than rendering
Greek into English. They were translating nonviolent
resistance into docility. Jesus did *not* tell his
oppressed hearers not to resist evil. That would have
been absurd. His entire ministry is utterly at odds
with such a preposterous idea. The Greek word is
made up of two parts: *anti*, a word still used in English
for "against," and *histēmi*, a verb which in its noun
form (*stasis*) means violent rebellion, armed revolt,
sharp dissention. Thus Barabbas is described as a
rebel "who had committed murder in the
insurrection" (Mark 15:7; Luke 23:19, 25), and the
townspeople in Ephesus "are in danger of being
charged with *rioting*" (Acts 19:40). The term generally
refers to a potentially lethal disturbance or armed
revolution.[11]

A proper translation of Jesus' teaching would then
be, "Do not strike back at evil (or, one who has done
you evil) in kind. Do not give blow for blow. Do not
retaliate against violence with violence." Jesus was
no less committed to opposing evil than the anti-
Roman resistance fighters. The only difference was
over the means to be used: *how* one should fight evil.

There are three general responses to evil: 1) passivity, 2) violent opposition, and 3) the third way of
militant nonviolence articulated by Jesus. Human
evolution has conditioned us for only the first two of
these responses: flight or fight. "Fight" had been the
cry of Galileans who had abortively rebelled against

Rome only two decades before Jesus spoke. Jesus and many of his hearers would have seen some of the two thousand of their countrymen crucified by the Romans along the roadsides. They would have known some of the inhabitants of Sepphoris (a mere three miles north of Nazareth) who had been sold into slavery for aiding the insurrectionists' assault on the arsenal there. Some also would live to experience the horrors of the war against Rome in 66–70 C.E., one of the ghastliest in human history. If the option "fight" had no appeal to them, their only alternative was "flight": passivity, submission, or, at best, a passive-aggressive recalcitrance in obeying commands. For them no third way existed. Submission or revolt spelled out the entire vocabulary of their alternatives to oppression.

Now we are in a better position to see why King James' faithful servants translated *antistēnai* as "resist not". The king would not want people concluding that they had any recourse against his or any other sovereign's unjust policies. Therefore the populace must be made to believe that there are *two* alternatives and only two: flight or fight. Either we resist not or we resist. And Jesus commands us, according to these king's men, to resist not. Jesus appears to authorize monarchical absolutism. Submission is the will of God. Most modern translations have meekly followed in that path.

Neither of these invidious alternatives has anything to do with what Jesus is proposing. It is important that we be utterly clear about this point before going on: *Jesus abhors both passivity and violence as responses to evil.* His is a third alternative not even touched by those options. *Antistēnai* may be translated variously as "Do not take up arms against evil," "Do not react reflexively to evil," "Do not let evil dictate the terms of your opposition." The Good News Bible (TEV) translates it helpfully: "Do not take revenge on someone who wrongs you." The word cannot be construed to mean submission.

Jesus clarifies his meaning by three brief examples. "If any one strikes you on the right cheek, turn to him the other also." Why the *right* cheek? How does one strike another on the right cheek anyway? Try it. A blow by the right fist in that right-handed world would land on the *left* cheek of the opponent. To strike the right cheek with the fist would require using the left hand, but in that society the left hand was used only for unclean tasks. Even to gesture with the left hand at Qumran carried the penalty of ten days penance (The Dead Sea Scrolls, 1 QS 7). The only way one could strike the right cheek with the right hand would be with the *back of the hand*. What we are dealing with here is unmistakably an insult, not a fistfight. The intention clearly is not to injure but to humiliate, to put someone in his or her "place." One normally did not strike a peer thus, and if one did the fine was exorbitant (4 zuz was the fine for a blow to a peer with a fist, 400 zuz for backhanding him; but to an underling, no penalty whatever— *Mishna, Baba Kamma* 8:1–6). A backhand slap was the normal way of admonishing inferiors. Masters backhanded slaves; husbands, wives; parents, children; men, women; Romans, Jews. One black African told me that during his youth white farmers still gave the backhand to disobedient workers.

We have here a set of unequal relations, in each of which retaliation would be suicidal. The only normal response would be cowering submission.

It is important to ask who Jesus' audience is. In

every case, Jesus' listeners are not those who strike, initiate lawsuits or impose forced-labor, but their victims ("If anyone strikes you...would sue you...forces you to go one mile..."). There are among his hearers people who were subjected to these very indignities, forced to stifle their inner outrage at the dehumanizing treatment meted out to them by the hierarchical system of caste and class, race and gender, age and status, and as a result of imperial occupation.

Why then does he counsel these already humiliated people to turn the other cheek? Because this action robs the oppressor of the power to humiliate. The person who turns the other cheek is saying, in effect, "Try again. Your first blow failed to achieve its intended effect. I deny you the power to humiliate me. I am a human being just like you. Your status (gender, race, age, wealth) does not alter that fact. You cannot demean me."

Such a response would create enormous difficulties for the striker. Purely logistically, how do you now hit the other cheek? You cannot backhand it with your right hand. If you hit with a fist, you make yourself an equal, acknowledging the other as a peer. But the whole point of the back of the hand is to reinforce the caste system and its institutionalized inequality. Even if you order the person flogged, the point has been irrevocably made. You have been forced, against your will, to regard that person as an equal human being. You have been stripped of your power to dehumanize the other.

The second example Jesus gives is set in a court of law. Someone is being sued for his outer garment.[12] Who would do that and under what circumstances? The Old Testament provides the clues.

If you lend money to any of my people with you *who is poor*, you shall not be to him as a creditor, and you shall not exact interest from him. If ever you take your neighbor's garment in pledge, you shall restore it to him before the sun goes down; for that is his only covering, it is his mantle for his body; in what else shall he sleep? And if he cries to me, I will hear, for I am compassionate. (Exod. 22:25–27)

When you make your neighbor a loan of any sort, you shall not go into his house to fetch his pledge. You shall stand outside, and the man to whom you make the loan shall bring the pledge out to you. *And if he is a poor man*, you shall not sleep in his pledge; when the sun goes down, you shall restore to him the pledge that he may sleep in his cloak and bless you...You shall not...take a widow's garment in pledge. (Deut. 24:10–13, 17)

They that trample the head of the poor into the dust of the earth...lay themselves down beside every altar upon garments taken in pledge...(Amos 2:7–8)

Only the poorest of the poor would have nothing but an outer garment to give as collateral for a loan. Jewish law strictly required its return every evening at sunset, for that was all the poor had in which to sleep. The situation to which Jesus alludes is one with which all his hearers would have been all too familiar: the poor debtor has sunk ever deeper into poverty, the debt cannot be repaid, and his creditor has hauled him into court to try to wring out repayment by legal means.

Indebtedness was the most serious social problem in first century Palestine. Jesus' parables are full of debtors struggling to salvage their lives. The situation was not, however, a natural calamity that had overtaken the incompetent. It was the direct consequence of Roman imperial policy. Emperors had taxed the wealthy so vigorously to fund their wars that the rich began seeking non-liquid investments to secure their wealth. Land was best, but there was a problem: it was not bought and sold on the open market as today but was ancestrally owned and passed down over generations. Little land was ever for sale, in Palestine at least. Exorbitant interest, however, could be used to drive landowners into ever deeper debt until they were forced to sell their land. By the time of Jesus we see this process already far advanced: large estates (*latifundia*) owned by absentee landlords, managed by stewards, and worked by servants, sharecroppers, and day laborers. It is no accident that the first act of the Jewish revolutionaries in 66 C.E. was to burn the Temple treasury, where the record of debts was kept.

It is in this context that Jesus speaks. His hearers are the poor ("if any one would sue *you*"). They share a rankling hatred for a system that subjects them to humiliation by stripping them of their lands, their goods, finally even their outer garments.

Why then does Jesus counsel them to give over their inner garment as well? This would mean stripping off all their clothing and marching out of court stark naked! Put yourself in the debtor's place, and imagine the chuckles this saying must have evoked. There stands the creditor, beet-red with embarrassment, your outer garment in the one hand, your underwear in the other. You have suddenly turned the tables on him. You had no hope of winning the trial; the law was entirely in his favor. But you have refused to be humiliated, and at the same time you have registered a stunning protest against a system that spawns such debt. You have said in effect, "You want my robe?

Here, take everything! Now you've got all I have except my body. Is that what you'll take next?"

Nakedness was taboo in Judaism, and shame fell not on the naked party, but on the person viewing or causing one's nakedness (Gen. 9:20–27). By stripping you have brought the creditor under the same prohibition that led to the curse of Canaan. As you parade into the street, your friends and neighbors, startled, aghast, inquire what happened. You explain. They join your growing procession, which now resembles a victory parade. The entire system by which debtors are oppressed has been publicly unmasked. The creditor is revealed to be not a "respectable" moneylender but a party in the reduction of an entire social class to landlessness and destitution. This unmasking is not simply punitive, however; it offers the creditor a chance to see, perhaps for the first time in his life, what his practices cause, and to repent.

Jesus in effect is sponsoring clowning. In so doing he shows himself to be thoroughly Jewish. A later saying of the Talmud runs, "If your neighbor calls you an ass, put a saddle on your back."[13]

The Powers That Be literally stand on their dignity. Nothing depotentiates them faster than deft lampooning. By refusing to be awed by their power, the powerless are emboldened to seize the initiative, even where structural change is not possible. This message, far from being a counsel of perfection unattainable in this life, is a practical, strategic measure for empowering the oppressed. It provides a hint of how to take on the entire system in a way that unmasks its essential cruelty and to burlesque its pretensions to justice, law, and order. Here is a poor man who will no longer be treated as a sponge to be squeezed dry by the rich. He accepts the laws as they stand, pushes them to the point of absurdity, and reveals them for what they really are. He strips nude, walks out before his compatriots, and leaves the creditor and the whole economic edifice which he represents, stark naked.

Was Johan Stander, the renegade South African nationalist businessman, thinking of this passage, or was he just fed up, when he removed his trousers in front of the Port Elizabeth city hall in April 1986, while demonstrating against apartheid?[14]

Jesus' third example, the one about going the second mile, is drawn from the very enlightened practice of limiting the amount of forced labor that Roman soldiers could levy on subject peoples. Jews would have seldom encountered legionnaires except in time of war or insurrection. It would have been auxiliaries who were headquartered in Judea, paid at half the rate of legionnaires and rather a scruffy bunch. In Galilee, Herod Antipas maintained an army patterned after Rome's; presumably they also had the right to impose labor. Mile markers were placed regularly beside the highways. A soldier could impress a civilian to carry his pack one mile only; to force the civilian to go farther carried with it severe penalties under military law. In this way Rome attempted to limit the anger of the occupied people and still keep its armies on the move. Nevertheless, this levy was a bitter reminder to the Jews that they were a subject people even in the Promised Land.

To this proud but subjugated people Jesus does not counsel revolt. One does not "befriend" the soldier, draw him aside, and drive a knife into his ribs. Jesus was keenly aware of the futility of armed revolt against Roman imperial might and minced no words about it, though it must have cost him support from the revolutionary factions.

But why walk the second mile? Is this not to rebound to the opposite extreme: aiding and abetting the enemy? Not at all. The question here, as in the two previous instances, is how the oppressed can recover the initiative, how they can assert their human dignity in a situation that cannot for the time being be changed. The rules are Caesar's, but not how one responds to the rules—that is God's, and Caesar has no power over that.

Imagine then the soldier's surprise when, at the next mile marker, he reluctantly reaches to assume his pack (sixty-five to eighty-five pounds in full gear), and you say, "Oh no, let me carry it another mile." Why would you do that? What are you up to? Normally he has to coerce your kinsmen to carry his pack, and now you do it cheerfully, and *will not stop!* Is this a provocation? Are you insulting his strength? Being kind? Trying to get him disciplined for seeming to make you go farther then you should? Are you planning to file a complaint? Create trouble?

From a situation of servile impressment, you have once more seized the initiative. You have taken back the power of choice. The soldier is thrown off-balance by being deprived of the predictability of your response. He has never dealt with such a problem before. Now you have forced him into making a decision for which nothing in his previous experience has prepared him. If he has enjoyed feeling superior to the vanquished, he will not enjoy it today. Imagine the hilarious situation of a Roman infantryman pleading with a Jew, "Aw, come on, please give me back my pack!" The humor of this scene may escape those who picture it through sanctimonious eyes, but it could scarcely have been lost on Jesus' hearers, who must have been regaled at the prospect of thus discomfitting their oppressors.

Some readers may object to the idea of discomfitting the soldier or embarrassing the creditor. But can people who are engaged in oppressive acts repent unless they are made uncomfortable with their actions? There is, admittedly, the danger of using nonviolence as a tactic of revenge and humiliation. There is also, at the opposite extreme, an equal danger of sentimentality and softness that confuses the uncompromising love of Jesus with being nice. Loving confrontation can free both the oppressed from docility and the oppressor from sin.

Even if nonviolent action does not immediately change the heart of the oppressor, it does affect those committed to it. As Martin Luther King, Jr. attested, it gives them new self-respect, and calls up resources of strength and courage they did not know they had. To those who have power, Jesus' advice to the powerless may seem paltry. But to those whose lifelong pattern has been to cringe, bow, and scrape before their masters, and who have internalized their role as inferiors, this small step is momentous. It is comparable to the attempt by black charwomen in South Africa to join together in what will be for some of them an almost insuperable step: to begin calling their employers by their first names.

These three examples amplify what Jesus means in his thesis statement: "Do not violently resist evil (or, one who is evil)." Instead of the two options engrained in us by millions of years of unreflective, brute response to biological threats from the environment: flight or fight, Jesus offers a third way. This new way marks a historic mutation in human development: the revolt against the principle of natural selection.[15] With Jesus a way emerges by which evil can be opposed without being mirrored:

Jesus' Third Way

Seize the moral initiative

Find a creative alternative to violence

Assert your own humanity and dignity as a person

Meet force with ridicule or humor

Break the cycle of humiliation

Refuse to submit or to accept the inferior position

Expose the injustice of the system

Take control of the power dynamic

Shame the oppressor into repentance

Stand your ground

Make the Powers make decisions for which they are not prepared

Recognize your own power

Be willing to suffer rather than retaliate

Force the oppressor to see you in a new light

Deprive the oppressor of a situation where a show of force is effective

Be willing to undergo the penalty of breaking unjust laws

Die to fear of the old order and its rules

Flight

Submission
Passivity
Withdrawal
Surrender

Fight

Armed revolt
Violent rebellion
Direct retaliation
Revenge

It is too bad that Jesus did not provide fifteen or twenty further examples, since we do not tend toward this new response naturally. Some examples from political history might help engrave it more deeply in our minds.

In Alagamar, Brazil, a group of peasants organized a long-term struggle to preserve their lands against attempts at illegal expropriation by national and international firms (with the connivance of local politicians and the military). Some of the peasants were arrested and jailed in town. Their companions decided they were all equally responsible, and hundreds marched to town and filled the house of the judge, demanding to be jailed with those who had been arrested. The judge was finally obliged to send them all home, including the prisoners.[16]

During the Vietnam War one woman claimed seventy-nine dependents on her income tax, all Vietnamese orphans, so she owed no tax. They were not legal dependents, of course, and were disallowed. No, she insisted, these children have been orphaned by indiscriminate United States bombing, and we are responsible for their lives. She forced the Internal Revenue Service to take her to court. That gave her a larger forum for making her case. She used the system against itself in order to unmask the moral indefensibility of what the system was doing. Of course she "lost" the case, but she made her point.

Another, one Jesus himself must have known and which may have served as a model for his examples: In 26 C.E., when Pontius Pilate brought the imperial standards into Jerusalem and displayed them at the Fortress Antonio overlooking the Temple, all Jerusalem was thrown into a tumult. These "effigies of Caesar which are called standards" not only infringed on the commandment against images but were the particular gods of the legions. Jewish leaders requested their removal. When Pilate refused, a large crowd of Jews "fell prostrate around his house and for five whole days and nights remained motionless in that position." On the sixth day, Pilate assembled the multitude in the stadium with the apparent intention of answering them. Instead, his soldiers surrounded the Jews in a ring three deep. As Josephus tells it,

> Pilate, after threatening to cut them down, if they refused to admit Caesar's images, signalled to the soldiers to draw their swords. Thereupon the Jews, as by concerted action, flung themselves in a body on the ground, extended their necks, and exclaimed that they were ready rather to die than to transgress the law. Overcome with astonishment at such intense religious zeal, Pilate gave orders for the immediate removal of the standards from Jerusalem.[17]

During World War II, when Nazi authorities in occupied Denmark promulgated an order that all Jews had to wear yellow armbands with the Star of David, the king made it a point to attend a celebration in the Copenhagen synagogue. His stand was affirmed by the Bishop of Sjaelland and other Lutheran clergy.[18] The Nazis eventually had to rescind the order.

It is important to repeat such stories in order to extend our imaginations for creative nonviolence. South Africa is teeming with examples. (Is anyone collecting them?) Since it is not a natural response, we need to be schooled in it. We need models, and we need to rehearse it in our daily lives if we ever hope to resort to it in crises.

Sadly, Jesus' three examples have been turned into laws, with no reference to the utterly changed contexts in which they were being applied. His attempt to nerve the powerless to assert their humanity under inhuman conditions has been turned into a legalistic prohibition on schoolyard fistfights between peers. Pacifists and those who reject pacifism alike have tended to regard Jesus' infinitely malleable insights as iron rules, the one group urging that they be observed inflexibly, the other treating them as impossible demands intended to break us and catapult us into the arms of grace. The creative, ironic, playful quality of Jesus' teaching has thus been buried under an avalanche of humorless commentary. And as always, the law kills.

How many a battered wife has been counseled, on the strength of a legalistic reading of this passage, to "turn the other cheek," when what she needs, according to the spirit of Jesus' words, is to find a way to restore her own dignity and end the vicious circle of humiliation, guilt, and bruising. She needs to assert some sort of control in the situation and force her husband to regard her as an equal, or get out of the relationship altogether. The victim needs to recover her self-worth and seize the initiative from her oppressor. And he needs to be helped to overcome his violence. The most creative and loving thing she could do, at least in the American setting, might be to have him arrested. "Turn the other cheek" is not intended as a legal requirement to be applied woodenly in every situation, but as the impetus for discovering creative alternatives that transcend the only two that we are conditioned to perceive: submission or violence, flight or fight.

Shortly after I was promoted from the "B" team to the varsity basketball squad in high school, I noticed that Ernie, the captain, was missing shot after shot from the corner because he was firing it like a bullet. So, helpfully I thought, I shouted, "Arch it, Ernie, arch it." His best friend, Ham, thought advice from a greenhorn impertinent and from that day on verbally sniped at me without letup. I had been raised a Christian, so I "turned the other cheek." To each sarcastic jibe I answered with a smile or soft words. This confused Ham somewhat; by the end of the season he lost his taste for taunts.

It was not until four years later that I suddenly woke to the realization that I had not loved Ham into changing. The fact was, *I hated his guts.* It might have been far more creative for me to have challenged him to a fistfight. Then he would have had to deal with me as an equal. But I was *afraid* to fight him, though the fight would probably have been a draw. I was scared I might get hurt. I was hiding behind the Christian "injunction" to "turn the other cheek," rather than asking, What is the most creative, transformative response to this situation? Perhaps I had done the right thing for the wrong reason, but I suspect that creative nonviolence can never be a genuinely moral response unless we are capable of first entertaining the possibility of violence and consciously saying No. Otherwise our nonviolence may actually be a mask for cowardice.

The oppressed of the third world are justifiably suspicious that we of the first world are more concerned with avoiding violence than with realizing justice. Nobel Peace Prize laureate Adolfo Peréz Esquivel comments, "What has always caught my attention is the attitude of peace movements in Europe and the United States, where nonviolence is envisioned as the final objective. Nonviolence is not the final objective. Nonviolence is a lifestyle. The final objective is humanity. It is life."[19]

Beyers Naude, when asked about the role of nonviolent direct action in South Africa today, responded that the churches long ago defaulted by failing to develop concrete strategies of militant nonviolence. The churches now must act decisively to develop such strategies and pay the full price in suffering and imprisonment. And, he concluded, we in the churches must not raise a single finger in judgment of those who have despaired of nonviolent change and have turned to violence as a last resort.

Ironically, in South Africa at this very moment, the apartheid regime is, by the stupidity of its brutal over-reactions to funeral processions and minor harrassments, helping to re-create a nonviolent movement among an oppressed people that had largely dismissed nonviolence as ineffectual. The issue is still undecided; an undisciplined and sporadic appeal to nonviolent direct action can quickly collapse when it is caught in the middle of violence from both sides. Any long-term nonviolent struggle must be disciplined, persistent, and broadly supported.

Perhaps it would help to juxtapose Jesus' teachings with Saul Alinsky's principles for nonviolent community action (in his *Rules for Radicals*[20]), so that we have a clearer sense of their practicality and pertinence to the struggles of our time. Among the rules Alinsky developed in his attempts to organize American workers and minority communities are these:

1. Power is not only what you have but what your enemy thinks you have.
2. Never go outside the experience of your people.
3. Wherever possible go outside the experience of the enemy.

Jesus recommended using one's experience of being belittled, insulted, or dispossessed (Alinsky's rule 2) in such a way as to seize the initiative from the oppressor, who finds the reaction of the oppressed totally outside his experience (second mile, stripping naked, turning the other cheek—3) and forces him or her to believe in your power (1) and perhaps even to recognize your humanity.

4. Make your enemies live up to their own book of rules.
5. Ridicule is your most potent weapon.
6. A good tactic is one that your people enjoy.
7. A tactic that drags on too long becomes a drag.

The debtor in Jesus' example turned the law against his creditor by obeying it (4)—and throwing in his underwear as well. The ruthlessness of the creditor is thus used as the momentum by which to expose his rapacity (5), and it is done quickly (7) and in a way that could only regale the debtor's sympathizers (6). All other such creditors are now put on notice, all other debtors armed with a new sense of possibilities.

8. Keep the pressure on.
9. The threat is usually more terrifying than the thing itself.

10. The major premise for tactics is the development of operations that will maintain a constant pressure upon the opposition.

Jesus, in the three brief examples he cites, does not lay out the basis of a sustained movement, but his ministry as a whole is a model of long-term social struggle (8, 10). Mark depicts Jesus' movements as a *blitzkrieg.* "Immediately" appears eleven times in chapter one alone. Jesus' teaching poses an immediate threat to the authorities. The good he brings is misperceived as evil, his following is overestimated, his militancy is misread as sedition, and his proclamation of the coming Reign of God is mistaken as a manifesto for military revolution (9). Disavowing violence, he wades into the hostility of Jerusalem openhanded, setting simple truth against force. Terrified by the threat of this man and his following, the authorities resort to their ultimate deterrent, death, only to discover it impotent and themselves unmasked. The cross, hideous and macabre, becomes the symbol of liberation. The movement that should have died becomes a world religion.

11. If you push a negative hard and deep enough it will break through to its counterside.
12. The price of a successful attack is a constructive alternative.
13. Pick the target, freeze it, personalize it, polarize it.

Alinsky delighted in using the most vicious behavior of his opponents—burglaries of movement headquarters, attempted blackmail, and failed assassinations—to destroy their public credibility.

Here were elected officials, respected corporations, and trusted police, engaging in patent illegalities in order to maintain privilege. In the same way, Jesus suggests amplifying an injustice (the other cheek, undergarment, second mile) in order to expose the fundamental wrongness of legalized oppression (11). The law is "compassionate" in requiring that the debtor's cloak be returned at sunset, yes; but Judaism in its most lucid moments knew that the whole system of usury and indebtedness was itself the root of injustice and should never have been condoned (Exod. 22:25). The restriction of enforced labor to carrying the soldier's pack a single mile was a great advance over unlimited impressment, but occupation troops had no right to be on Jewish soil in the first place. Jesus' teaching is a kind of moral jujitsu, a martial art for using the momentum of evil to throw it, but it requires penetrating beneath the conventions of legality to issues of fundamental justice and hanging onto them with dogged persistence. As Gandhi put it, "We are sunk so low that we fancy that it is our duty and religion to do what the law lays down." If people will only realize that it is cowardly to obey laws that are unjust, he continued, no one's tyranny will enslave them.[21]

Picking the target, freezing it, personalizing it, and polarizing it are the means, then, by which intensity is focused and brought to bear (13). For example, infant formula merchants were discouraging breast feeding and promoting their product in countries where women could not afford the powder. Often the parents overdiluted the formula causing malnutrition, or mixed it with unsanitary water resulting in diarrhea and death. But you cannot fight all the merchants of infant formula in the third world at once;

so you pick the biggest and most visible, Nestlé, even though doing so is technically unfair, since their competition gets off scot free. The focus pays off, however. Nestlé's recalcitrance leads to world-wide outrage and an international boycott. To avoid similar treatment most of the infant formula manufacturers make some changes. Eventually the boycott leader, the Infant Formula Action Coalition (INFACT), in conjunction with the World Health Organization and the United Nations International Children's Fund, draws up a code regulating the marketing of infant formula. In 1984, after eight years of struggle, Nestlé finally signs an agreement promising to comply with the new standards. And the whole campaign has been instigated out of an office the size of a closet.[22]

Jesus' constructive alternative (12) was, of course, the Reign of God. Turning the tables on one's oppressor may be fun now and then, but long-term structural and spiritual change requires an alternative vision. As the means of purveying that vision and living it in the midst of the old order, Jesus established a new counter-community that developed universalistic tendencies, erupting out of his own Jewish context and finally beyond the Roman Empire.

Jesus was not content merely to empower the powerless, however, and here his teachings fundamentally transcend Alinsky's. Jesus' sayings about non-retaliation are of one piece with his challenge to love our enemies. That theme will be the topic of Chapter Four. Here it is enough to remark that Jesus did not advocate nonviolence merely as a technique for outwitting the enemy, but as a just means of opposing the enemy in such a way as to hold open the possibility of the enemy's becoming just as well. Both sides must win. We are summoned to pray for our enemies' transformation, and to respond to ill-treatment with a love which is not only godly but also, I am convinced, can only be found in God.

To Alinsky's list I would like to add another "rule" of my own: Never adopt a strategy that you would not want your opponents to use against you. I would not object to my opponents using nonviolent direct actions against me, since such a move would require them to be committed to suffer and even die rather than resort to violence against me. It would mean that they would have to honor my humanity, believe that God can transform me, and treat me with dignity and respect. One of the ironies of nonviolence, in fact, is that those who depend on violent repression to defend their privileges *cannot* resort to nonviolence. There is something essentially contradictory between crushing the dissent of a society's victims and being willing to give one's life for justice and the truth.

There are also particular tactics which, while technically nonviolent, would break the Golden Rule. I would not, for example, condone invading a party held for the children of top executives of a corporation which we oppose and throwing balloons filled with skunk-scented water, or paint-bombing the home of a non-supportive bishop and slashing his tires, as one militant group of Christian activists did in the Pittsburgh area.[23]

Today we can draw on the cumulative historical experience of nonviolent social struggle over the centuries and employ newer tools for political and social analysis. But the spirit, the thrust, the surge for creative transformation which is the ultimate principle of the universe, is the same we see incarnated in Jesus. Freed from literalistic legalism, his teaching reads like a practical manual for empowering the powerless to seize the initiative even in situations impervious to change. It seems almost as if his teaching has only now, in this generation, become an inescapable task and practical necessity.

To people dispirited by the enormity of the injustices which crush us and the intractability of those in positions of power, Jesus' words beam hope across the centuries. We need not be afraid. We can reassert our human dignity. We can lay claim to the creative possibilities that are still ours, burlesque the injustice of unfair laws, and force evil out of hiding from behind the facade of legitimacy.

To risk confronting the Powers with such harlequinesque vulnerability, simultaneously affirming our own humanity and that of those whom we oppose, and daring to draw the sting of evil by absorbing it in our own bodies—such behavior is not likely to attract the faint of heart. But I am convinced that there is a whole host of people simply waiting for the Christian message to challenge them, for once, to a heroism worthy of their lives. Has Jesus not provided us with that word?

The Pragmatic Case for Jesus' Third Way in South Africa

Chapter Three

Once we determine that Jesus' Third Way is not a perfectionistic avoidance of violence but a creative struggle to restore the humanity of all parties in a dispute, the legalism that has surrounded this issue becomes unnecessary. We cannot sit in judgment over the responses of others to their oppression. Jesus' cleansing of the Temple was, by any honest reading of the text, a fairly violent act, even if it caused no casualties. According to Mark it was premeditated, not a sudden fit of pique (Mark 11:11, 15–19). Gandhi continually reiterated that if a person could not act nonviolently in a situation, violence was preferable to submission. "Where there is only a choice between cowardice and violence, I would advise violence."[24]

The reality of the South African situation is that government violence has already reached a scale that is intolerable for an increasing number of blacks. A soldier on leave confessed to his pastor his terrible guilt and conflict over carrying out an order to load an armored vehicle with rocks, drive into the black area, and throw the rocks at the people and their homes. When youths threw the rocks back, he and the other troops were ordered to open fire. (Apparently it never occurred to him, nor had he been taught by his church, that he could refuse the order and take the consequences.)

A six-year-old black, living illegally in church-owned white university housing, saw an armored personnel carrier ("Casspir") rumbling through his white neighborhood and dashed out into the street shouting, "Amandla! Amandla! Shoot me! Shoot me!" His mother rushed out and hustled him indoors. Had this occurred in a black neighborhood, the soldiers might have obliged him.

It is to their everlasting credit that black youth have shaken off the fear of death and the Powers that has so long paralyzed their parents. There is something holy in their rage, a cry for life that will no longer be denied, even at the cost of death. Nor do I think anyone can deny that this fearlessness has been one of the greatest inducements to make the government change.

There comes a point when a government has squandered too many chances to repent. After that, responsibility for the violence it engenders, even in its most hideous excesses, must be laid at the government's feet. We may fault the rock throwing of youth as ineffectual. We may wish their energies could be channeled into organized and disciplined actions in concert with entire communities. But the government's policy of detaining every emerging community leader, especially those who espouse nonviolence, makes such organizing incredibly difficult (though it is being done). We grieve over the "necklacing," the murder of government informers and collaborators and appointees, and the burning of their houses or stores. There are other, better ways to handle such traitors, and the violence against them has now provoked a counter-counter-violence far more insidious than that of the white troops and police: black vigilantes, encouraged and equipped and given carte blanche by the government to decimate active resistance in the townships and homelands. However deplorable this desperate violence of the oppressed becomes, it is the apartheid system that is its cause, and the acolytes of apartheid must answer for it.

It is not to these youth, who are like a forest fire out of control, that Jesus' Third Way needs to be addressed right now. They are like human torches by the light of whose immolation older generations of blacks and even some whites have at last perceived their own duty. It is rather to the adults, and most especially to black and white Christians, that Jesus' words bear a desperate and perhaps final relevance.

Jesus' Third Way is relevant in part for entirely pragmatic reasons. The military wing of the African National Congress (ANC) is not going to ride into Pretoria victoriously on the turrets of tanks. No one we talked with—not one—believes the ANC can win, or even wants, a hot war. The ANC has even shown remarkable restraint in the use of sabotage. There were only 136 "terror incidents" in 1985, up from a mere forty-four in 1984—still far short of an all-out sabotage campaign.[25] How easy it would be for blacks to pick off whites on lonely roads all over the country. Yet this virtually never happens. Whites spoke in sensationalist terms about the "huge caches" of weapons in the townships. Why, if this is so, did blacks launch only twenty-nine grenades in an entire year (1985), or so seldom return Casspir fire with AK-47s or rockets?[26]

The fact is that the black community is still virtually unarmed. Nor is there much likelihood that it will become adequately armed in the near future. The government's spy and informer network is ubiquitous. Even if blacks could be armed, the sheer logistical difficulty of supplying them across the huge expanse of South African territory precludes their ever being sufficiently equipped for even urban guerrilla warfare.

Hot war also would provide elements in the armed forces and security police license for genocidal and indiscriminate attacks on townships and homelands by tanks and Mirage jets. The South African government has one of the best-equipped armies in the world. As an unintended consequence of the international arms blockade, South Africa has become virtually self-sufficient in weapons production and has even become a vigorous exporter of military hardware. Its armed forces are thus impervious to further international sanctions, short of the collapse of the entire economy. Defense expenditures have skyrocketted. The whole of white society has been militarized. There are right-wingers who have opted for a Hitlerian "final solution," and are already seeing it implemented piecemeal and sporadically through unprovoked police violence and vigilante action in black areas.

The dream of violent revolution in South Africa is an opium vision with no basis in reality. The seduction of violence is its counterfeit offer of a quick fix. "If only we could blow up all the government leaders in their cabinet meeting." Yes, and they would be replaced by characters even more hard-line and unyielding, as the assassinated Prime Minister Verwoerd was succeeded by the crew that has produced the present emergency.[27] "For we are not contending against flesh and blood, but against the principalities, against the powers, against the world rulers of this present darkness" (Eph. 6:12). It is not the advocates but the very spirit of apartheid itself that must be killed. And it will only die as white South Africans are forced to recognize the humanity of those they have oppressed. That will only come about, as King so eloquently testified by word and example, through acts of sacrificial love which absorb the violence of the oppressors without turning it back on them. The blacks of South Africa have already proven countless times that they are capable of such courageous behavior. What has been lacking so far is resolute training and leadership by the churches.

Even if armed revolt were possible, can anyone argue cogently that the result of total war in South Africa would be an era of justice and peace? Even campaigns of civil disobedience foster a degree of contempt for law by those who do not grasp its basic commitment to a society founded on law. The anarchy of all-out civil war would bring with it a total collapse of public services, protection, food distribution, transportation, and communication.

There is another, altogether ironic deception involved in the glorification of violence. It can be a cop-out on active resistance. We actually saw this happening in several places. Black students insisted that nonviolence had failed and only violence would work. But they were not off on the borders of Namibia or Mozambique fighting for the South West African People's Organization (SWAPO) or the military wing of the ANC. And since they believe nonviolence is ineffective, they are not engaged in local actions against apartheid either. They mouthed the rhetoric of violence but were busy with studies that will help them get ahead while others pay the price. This has led to guilt and cynicism. They had, in effect, staked all their hopes on a military victory at the borders which will never come until people like themselves make the urban centers ungovernable. Armed revolution is utterly dependent on civil unrest in the heart of the country, and that is precisely what these students were avoiding. Radical chic talk about violence was merely, in their case, a convenient cover for doing nothing.

Clergy, too, sometimes used the necessity of violence to justify their not espousing a nonviolent line. Then they would always add the qualifier, "Though of course I could never bring myself to kill someone." So they have it both ways. They do not "believe" in nonviolence, and they cannot "conceive" of violence. What a deft recipe for inaction!

Jesus' way, which is the way of the cross, means voluntarily taking on the violence of the state, and that will mean casualties. But they will be nowhere near the scale that would result from violent revolution. It is a never-ending source of amazement to me that people conclude from the Sharpeville massacre that the only alternative is violence. The death toll there was sixty-nine, a tragic figure, yet still far less than one might expect from a single skirmish in open warfare. (It is generally forgotten that the shooting was precipitated by a small group of rock throwers, quite possibly agents provocateurs, who broke the strict discipline that seven thousand demonstrators had maintained through several hours of police harassment.)

Britain's Indian colony of three hundred million people was liberated nonviolently at a cost of about eight thousand lives, that is, 1 in 40,000. In terms of South Africa's population this is eight hundred lives. The British apparently suffered not a single casualty, dead or wounded.[28] It took twenty-seven years (1919-1946). France's Algerian colony of about ten million was later liberated in seven years (1955-61) by violence, but it cost almost one million lives, that is, 1 in 10 (or three million in terms of South Africa's population). The staggering differential in lives lost certainly cannot be ascribed to the French being more barbaric or determined to keep their colony than the British. And the French were fighting merely to keep a colony; white South Africans would be fighting for their native soil.

Solidarity in Poland (population thirty-seven million) nonviolently stood up to the ruthless power of a communist government and lost about three hundred lives over a period of three years. About the same time Argentina, in a violent but fruitless effort to take the Falkland/Malvinas Islands, lost something like one thousand lives in two weeks against the democratic British.[29]

In the United States civil rights struggle, about fifty thousand demonstrators were jailed, but fewer than one hundred of those engaged in campaigns were killed.[30] By contrast, armed revolution in Cuba cost twenty thousand lives, in Nicaragua twenty thousand. Already in El Salvador, sixty thousand civilians have died, quite apart from military casualties; and there is no end in sight. Over the past thirty years one hundred thousand Guatemalans have lost their lives, out of a population of only 7.8 million. South Africa's war in Namibia is estimated to have already cost ten thousand lives. The South African Defense Force lost two thousand to twenty-five hundred troops there (including accidents and disease) between 1975 and 1983, a higher casualty rate proportionately than the United States suffered in Vietnam.[31] We cannot ignore the implications of these statistics, for *the comparative degree of carnage is a moral issue.*

The ANC abandoned nonviolence after only eight years of concerted nonviolent direct action (1952-1960)—not to be confused with earlier efforts at "negotiation" and sporadic acts of passive resistance. Was that abandonment premature? The old refrain, "We tried nonviolence for fifty years (read 'eight') and it didn't work" should now be replaced by another: "We have tried violent resistance for twenty-seven years and have very little to show for it."

We need to be very clear that it is in the government's interest to make people believe that nonviolence does not work. The security forces chafe at the few restraints still imposed on them. They long for occasions to use the full force of their massive power in knockout blows. Nonviolent actions do not supply them with that pretext and are thus a source of endless frustration. For that reason, the South African government has repeatedly used its own secret agents to provoke violence, which can then be managed easily by the regime's superior firepower. After seven years in prison for working in the revolutionary underground, the Afrikaner poet Breyten Breytenbach himself had second-thoughts: "Have we veritably thought *through* all the negative connotations and results of armed struggle, and the dangers to the political ideas, which we cherish, of underground work itself? Isn't it very often just a Boy Scout game?"[32]

Nonviolence also faces a double standard. If a single

43

case can be shown where it does not work, nonviolence as a whole can then be discredited. No such rigorous standard is applied to violence, which regularly fails to achieve its goals. Close to two-thirds of all governments that assume power by means of coups d'état are ousted by the same means; only 1 in 20 post-coup governments gives way to a civil government.[33]

The issue, however, is not just which *works* better, but also which *fails* better. While a nonviolent strategy also does not always "work" in terms of preset goals—though in another sense it always "works"—at least the casualties and destruction are far less severe. The armed revolt in Hungary was crushed by the Soviets at the cost of five to six thousand Hungarian lives; forty thousand were imprisoned, tortured or detained. In Czechoslovakia, where a spontaneous nonviolent resistance was mounted, seventy died, and political prisoners were *released*.

The tragedy is that some black youth earnestly believe liberation is just a few more thrown stones away. The white-heat of their rebelliousness has already kindled conflicts with their elders, who have in many cases lost all control of their children, and are no longer treated with respect. That wild energy must be offered constructive channels quickly, or it will destroy what is left of an already apartheid-decimated family and community life.

I do not believe that the churches can adequately atone for their past inaction simply by baptizing revolutionary violence under the pretext of just war theory. No war in that setting could be called just, given the inevitable level of casualties and atrocities, when a concerted nonviolent struggle has not yet been resolutely attempted.

Nonviolent revolutions never happen by accident. They are the outcome of grassroots training, discipline, organizing, and hard work. Beneath the rhetoric of violence-talk lies another reality in South Africa today: the Third Way *is* being both taught and practiced. Most elements comprising the United Democratic Front (UDF), students' organizations, women's organizations, and the labor movement are at least publicly nonviolent and discipline those who step beyond it. Why then have church leaders not been more vocal and consistent in their support of Jesus' Third Way?

The Theological Case for Jesus' Third Way in South Africa

Chapter Four

So far I have presented only pragmatic reasons for the use of nonviolence in the South African struggle. For the Christian, however, there are deeper and finally ultimate grounds for opting for Jesus' way.

One: The Love of Enemies

Jesus' Third Way bears at its very heart the love of enemies. This is the hardest word to utter in the South African context, because it can so easily be misunderstood as spinelessness. But it is precisely the message King made central to his efforts in similarly polarized circumstances in the American South.

> To our most bitter opponents we say: We shall match your capacity to inflict suffering by our capacity to endure suffering. We shall meet your physical force with soul force. Do to us what you will, and we shall continue to love you. We cannot in all good conscience obey your unjust laws, because noncooperation with evil is as much a moral obligation as is cooperation with good. Throw us in jail, and we shall still love you. Bomb our homes and

threaten our children, and we shall still love you. Send your hooded perpetrators of violence into our communities at the midnight hour and beat us and leave us half dead, and we shall still love you. But be ye assured that we will wear you down by our capacity to suffer. One day we shall win freedom, but not only for ourselves. We shall so appeal to your heart and conscience that we shall win you in the process, and our victory will be a double victory.[34]

It cannot be stressed too much: love of enemies has, for our time, become the litmus test of authentic Christian faith. Commitment to justice, liberation, or the overthrow of oppression is not enough, for all too often the means used have brought in their wake new injustices and oppressions. Love of enemies is the recognition that the enemy, too, is a child of God. The enemy too believes he or she is in the right, and fears us because we represent a threat against his or her values, lifestyle, and affluence. When we demonize our enemies, calling them names and identifying them with absolute evil, we deny that they have that of God within them which still makes transformation possible. We play God. We write them out of the Book of Life. We conclude that our enemy has drifted beyond the redemptive hand of God.

I submit that the ultimate religious question today should no longer be the Reformation's "How can I find a gracious God?" It should be instead, "How can I find God in my enemy?" What guilt was for Luther, the enemy has become for us: the goad that can drive us to God. What has formerly been a purely private affair—justification by faith through grace—has now, in our age, grown to embrace the world. As John Stoner comments, we can no more save ourselves from our enemies than we can save ourselves from sin, but God's amazing grace offers to save us from both.[35] There is, in fact, no other way to God for our time but through the enemy, for loving the enemy has become the key both to human survival in the nuclear age and to personal transformation. Either we find the God who causes the sun to rise on the evil and on the good, or we may have no more sunrises.

Of course it is difficult, even seemingly impossible, to forgive those who have killed members of your family, or tortured you, or sold out to the authorities. Yet this kind of behavior is nothing new. It is one of the rules of the power game that the oppressor always uses the maximum force possible within existing political and military constraints. It is little wonder then that people tend to feel that their own suffering is exceptional; it always is. Did not Jesus himself, and thousands of Christians all through the ages, experience the same? It is our very inability to love our enemies that throws us into the arms of grace. What law was for Luther, the enemy has become for us. It is precisely here, in the midst of persecution, that many will find themselves overtaken by the miraculous power of divine forgiveness. God's forgiving love can burst like a flare even in the night of our grief and hatred and free us to love. It is in just such times as these, when forgiveness seems impossible, that the power of God most mightily can manifest itself. There is a subtle pride in clinging to our hatreds as justified, as if our enemies had passed beyond even God's capacity to love and forgive, as if no one in human history had known sufferings greater than ours, as if Jesus' sufferings were inadequate and puny alongside what we must face.

To a certain extent the refusal to love enemies is a result of seeing the opposition as a monolith. We fail to note that the enemy camp is inevitably riddled with power struggles, fragmentation, back-stabbing, personal vendettas, bureaucratic infighting, and careerism, all of which conspire to prevent maximum efficiency in oppression. Likewise, we tend to freeze them in their current public postures, denying that they can make the very changes we are demanding of them. How can we conceive of a just and nonracial South Africa for the future unless the whites now in the grip of racism somehow can be liberated from its hold? In 1980 over forty percent of employed Afrikaners were on the payroll of state or parastate institutions. Many of them operate the apartheid apparatus and therefore have a direct interest in the status quo. The security police are recruited almost exclusively from the poorer and rural sectors of Afrikaner society. Unless these people are to be exterminated in a genocidal race war, they must be converted. And no one can show others the error that is within them, as Thomas Merton wisely remarked, unless the others are convinced that their critic first sees and loves the good that is within them.[36]

Love of enemies is, in the broadest sense, behaving out of one's own deepest self-interest: "that you may be sons and daughters of your Father who is in heaven" (Matt. 5:45). It is in my own self-interest to recognize that my opponents have jobs or mortgaged houses that tie them to the existing economic and political system. They are afraid they are losing their grip on the world. They need to be reassured that revolution will not strip them of all means of making a livelihood or all their hard-won security. Likewise, they need to be reassured continually, as blacks generally have been doing, that there will be a place for them in the new society being born.

The fact is that white views in South Africa are

changing. A summer 1986 poll by the *Sunday Times* of London found that forty-five percent of whites are unhappy with apartheid, up from thirty-two percent a year before. Fifty-six percent favored freeing Nelson Mandela, and seventy-two percent say they expect the apartheid system to be gone in ten years (up from sixty-three percent last year).[37]

We need to realize also the degree to which politicians refuse to change in order to save face, to avoid the appearance of backing down under pressure. For this reason, Gandhi always attempted to keep the demands of his campaigns specific to the local situation and to convince his opponents that the struggle was not for a victory over them but simply for fundamental justice. Once, having filled the jails over the right of untouchables to use the Nykom Temple Road, and finally securing their right to use it, Gandhi-led demonstrators refrained from using the road for a period of months. This provided the Brahmans and authorities a space in which to save face and back down without seeming to have capitulated. Gandhi distinguished between the "nonviolence of the weak," which uses harassment to break the opponent, and the "nonviolence of the strong" (what he called *satyagraha* or "truth force"), which seeks the opponent's good by freeing him or her from oppressive actions.[38]

King so imbued this understanding of Jesus' Third Way into his followers that it became the ethos of the entire civil rights movement. One evening, during the turbulent weeks when Selma, Alabama was the focal point of civil rights struggle, the large crowd of black and white activists standing outside the Ebenezer Baptist Church was electrified by the sudden arrival of a black funeral home operator from Montgomery.

He reported that a group of black students demonstrating near the capitol just that afternoon had been surrounded by police on horseback, all escape barred, and cynically commanded to disperse or take the consequences. Then the mounted police waded into the students and beat them at will. Police prevented ambulances from reaching the injured for two hours. Our informant was the driver of one of those ambulances and he had driven straight to Selma to tell us about it.

The crowd outside the church seethed with rage. Cries went up, "Let's march!" Behind us, across the street, stood, rank on rank, the Alabama State Troopers and the local police forces of Sheriff Jim Clark. The situation was explosive. A young black minister stepped to the microphone and said, "It's time we sang a song." He opened with the line, "Do you love Martin King?" to which those who knew the song responded, "Certainly, Lord!" "Do you love Martin King?" "Certainly, Lord!" "Do you love Martin King?" "Certainly, certainly, certainly Lord!" Right through the chain of command of the Southern Christian Leadership Conference he went, the crowd each time echoing, warming to the song, "Certainly, certainly, certainly Lord!" Without warning he sang out, "Do you love Jim Clark?"—the Sheriff?! "Cer...certainly, Lord" came the stunned, halting reply. "Do you love Jim Clark?" "Certainly, Lord"—it was stronger this time. "Do you love Jim Clark?" Now the point had sunk in, as surely as Amos' in chapters 1 and 2: "Certainly, certainly, certainly Lord!"

Rev. James Bevel then took the mike. We are not just fighting for our rights, he said, but for the good of the whole society. "It's not enough to defeat Jim Clark—do you hear me Jim?—we want you converted. We cannot win by hating our oppressors. We have to love them into changing."

And Jim Clark did change. When the voter registration drive in Selma was concluded, Jim Clark realized that he could not be re-elected without the black vote. He began courting black voters. Later he even confessed, and I believe sincerely, that he had been wrong in his bias against blacks.

King enabled his followers to see the white racist also as a victim of the Principalities and Powers, in this case the whole ethos of the Southern Way of Life. Southern racists also needed to be changed. This provided a space and grace for transformation. While much more remains to be done in America than any of us likes to think, change has occurred, datable to events like these, when the tide of racial fury was stemmed by the willingness of a few people to absorb its impact in their own bodies and to allow it to spread no farther.

An argument once heard in Latin America, and now being revived in South Africa, is that while nonviolence is certainly the Biblical norm, it can be used only against governments which have achieved a minimum moral level. It can work with the genial British in India but not with the violent defenders of apartheid or the brutal communists. This argument has been exploded by events, however, since the Poles and the Czechs have both demonstrated that nonviolence can in fact be used against ruthless regimes. And as for the British in India, they were no more genial than the Romans in Palestine. Had Jesus waited for the Romans to achieve a minimum moral level, he never would have been able to articulate the message of nonviolence to begin with. On the contrary, his teaching does not presuppose a threshold of decency, but that of God in everyone. There is no one, and surely no entire people, in whom the image of God has been utterly extinguished. Faith in God means believing that *anyone* can be transformed, regardless of the past. To write off whole groups of people as intrinsically racist and violent is to accept the very same premise that upholds apartheid. That argument is used to support wholesale discrimination against blacks: blacks are not quite human, a different species altogether. The moment we argue that the South African defenders of apartheid are morally inferior beings, we reduce ourselves to their moral level. We become no different in kind than Nazis who claimed that Jews were racially inferior, or white supremacists in America who insist that blacks or Native Americans are animals or savages. As Narayan Desai remarks, "Non-violence presupposes a level of humanness—however low it may be, in every human being."[39]

In the final analysis, then, love of enemies is trusting God for miracles. If God can forgive, redeem, and transform me, I must also believe that God can work such wonders with anyone. Love of enemies is seeing one's oppressors through the prism of the Reign of God—not only as they now are but also as they can become: totally transformed by the power of God. As Milan Machovec put it—and perhaps it took a Marxist who rediscovered Jesus to say it with such clarity:

> The enemy must be resisted in so far as he serves the power of darkness, although it would be better to say that the power of darkness should be resisted rather than the enemy. He should be seen not as the servant of darkness but as someone who is capable of a future conversion. Therefore, though he uses evil means—

despotism, the sword, force, darkness—one must not answer him with these same means. If one answered him in kind, with lies, deceit, violence and force, one would be denying oneself and him the future and the possibility of change, one would be perpetuating the kingdom of evil. [40]

Two: The Means are Commensurate with the New Order

Jesus' Third Way uses means commensurate with the new order we desire. Violent struggles are necessarily hierarchical; all warfare inevitably is. This pattern of centralized power-holding is not easily renounced after victory is won. After assuming power, ideological differences within the movement are dealt with by the same methods used to gain power: exterminations, purges, torture, and mass arrests. Revolutions must, in the nature of things, depend on men and women who have exercised their critical faculties. But insofar as the revolution's ideal is to create a society unanimous in its beliefs and wholly free from internal conflict, it must, if successful, destroy the very critical tendencies that made its success possible.

A rule of terror characterized the successful emergence to office of Stalin, Mao, Bella (Algeria), Khomeini, and Pinochet. Stalin's attempts to control his real and imagined enemies led to the extermination of twenty million Soviet citizens—as many of them as were killed in World War II. In attempting to "protect the revolution," one Yugoslav commented, he "killed more good communists than the bourgeoisie of the whole world put together."[41]

Even Castro arrested and left to rot those among his closest compatriots in the guerrilla struggle who dared to criticize his policies as prime minister. Such purges cost a new government its best leadership, lead to middle-class and professional flight, establish the security police at the heart of the nation's life, and undermine its recovery. Once the path of violence has been chosen, it cannot be easily renounced even in the new regime. In John Swomley's words, violence is "not conducive for teaching the respect for persons on which democracy depends."[42]

By contrast, nonviolent revolution is not a program for seizing power. It is, says Gandhi, a program for transforming relationships, ending in a peaceful transfer of power. When elements of the Indian Congress proposed resorting to violence on one occasion, Gandhi replied, "We've come a long way with the British. When they eventually leave we want them to do so as friends."[43] This attitude of respect for the opponent requires keeping the dialogue open. That demands courage. It also helps reduce the paranoia that builds from being under continual surveillance. Upon his release from detainment in 1985, Richard Steele, an organizer of the End Conscription Campaign, continued to be followed by his interrogators. They would be parked outside his apartment in the mornings. Instead of ignoring them or trying to shake them off his trail, he made it a practice to go over and speak with them. This made them very nervous. Their explicit purpose was intimidation, and now they were forced to speak to this man who refused to be cowed. By insisting on treating them as human beings, he was challenging them to become who they will be in the Reign of God.

Violence simply is not radical enough, since it generally changes only the actors but not the way power is exercised.

Three: Respect for the Rule of Law

Jesus' Third Way preserves respect for the rule of law even in the act of resisting oppressive laws. Violent revolutionaries are involved in a contradiction that jeopardizes the very order they wish to establish. They plan to gain power by the very means that they will declare illegal when they gain power. But they will have established a precedent that legitimates the use of violence by those who disagree with them and wish to replace them. Since they will not have fostered democracy in their rise to power, they can only resort to force in silencing their opposition.

King's insight was that blacks, if they wished to achieve a share of the American Dream, could not begin by destroying the institutions and violating that respect for law which were the source of the benefits they sought. We want a society freed from every last vestige of apartheid, but at the same time we also want a society where people still stop for traffic lights, where robbers are apprehended, and where gangs of lawless ruffians are not free to roam the streets. In the civil disobedience practiced by King and Gandhi, a person in the very act of appealing to a higher moral authority subjects himself or herself to the principle of civil law. No proponent of the Third Way would ever attempt to get off scot-free for breaking an unjust law, for that would encourage the chaos of lawlessness in a society already rendered intolerable by legalized injustices. Civil disobedience always must be engaged in with deep respect for the idea of law. Indeed, it is voluntary submission to the due penalty of the law that discourages frivolous violations.

Anxiety over lawlessness lies behind certain complaints of black parents who see some black youths setting themselves up as the law, enforcing boycotts without democratic procedures or larger community involvement, and becoming inflated by their own first taste of corrupting power. Citing Romans 13:1–7 and its call to "submit to the governing authorities" is no answer, however, unless we are clear about its meaning.

First, "submit" does not imply blind obedience. As the report, "Obedience, Submission and Civil Disobedience" of the Presbyterian Church of Southern Africa points out, submission may lead to obedience but does not necessarily require it. Jesus was subject to his parents (Luke 2:51) but refused to obey his own mother's command (Mark 3:31–35). All things are subjected to Christ (Eph. 1:20–22) but they do not yet all obey him. Jesus subjected himself to Jewish law, yet he deliberately broke it where it violated his discernment of God's will. Yet he whom the church would later declare greater than the law submitted to its penalties for his disobedience. So too, Peter and John stated before the Sanhedrin, "Whether it is right in the sight of God to listen to you rather than to God, you must judge; for we cannot but speak of what we have seen and heard" (Acts 4:19).

Secondly, Romans 13:2 has been translated in such a way that all resistance even to the most satanic despotism appears to be prohibited. The Revised Standard Version is representative: "Therefore he who resists the authorities resists what God has appointed, and those who resist will incure judgment." The first term for "resist," *antitassō*, is a military term meaning literally, "to range in battle against," "to post in adverse array, as an army," "to set oneself in armed opposition." The second and third instances of "resist" in the same sentence are our old friend from Matthew 5:39, *anthistēmi*. It too indicates armed insurrection, violent resistance. Romans 13:1–7 is not, then an injuction against all forms of resistance to an unjust regime, but only *armed* resistance. Romans 13:2 might then be translated, "Therefore the person who engages in armed revolt against the political system commits insurrection against what God has ordained." God wills that there be political order and not chaos. Human life is intolerable apart from the rule of law.

Thirdly, this rule is to be for the benefit of all. The ruler "is God's servant for your good" (Rom. 13:4). What happens when that rule is no longer good for the majority of the people? Romans 13 only tells us how government *ought* to be, as Allan Boesak reminds us. Revelation 13 tells us how government ought *not* to be. "The servant of God can very easily become the beast."[44] Even when the government is in a state of apostasy and rebellion against God, however, the Christian is still encouraged to struggle against it nonviolently (Rev. 13:10).

We too should, following Jesus, refuse ever to obey an unjust law. But by undergoing its recoil against us, we affirm our willingness to suffer on behalf of a higher law which we are determined to see transform the law of the land. We are lawful in our illegality. It is only because we submit to the principle of law that we demand that unjust laws be made just in the first place.

It is true that South African blacks have been deprived of participating in formulating the laws that govern them. But this is no grounds for declaring the government wholly illegitimate. The Biblical understanding of the Powers is that they are indeed fallen but not totally depraved. Even when they are repressive in the extreme, they still embody something that must be honored and to which we must subject ourselves: the *principle* of law. Romans 13, however misused by oppressors, articulates this fundamental truth. We must begin from a basis of legality in order to foster a new society which will abide by the letter and the spirit of just laws.

Four: Rooting out the Violence

Jesus' Third Way requires us to root out the violence within our own souls. To resist something, we must meet it with counter-force. If we resist violence with violence, we simply mirror back its evil. We become what we resist. But even when we resist evil creatively, seizing the initiative and lovingly challenging the Powers to change, there is danger.

The easiest temptation to unmask is self-righteousness. What a wonderfully expansive feeling it is to denounce evil grandly, especially an evil so unequivocal as apartheid! What a host of oversights and sins are covered by such greasy goodness, how nice we feel about ourselves. In such a mood it is easy to fall into us/them thinking, to forget our own complicity in or past complacency toward the evil we now so tardily (always, it seems, tardily) oppose. During such seizures of summer saintliness it is virtually impossible not to demonize the enemy; indeed, part of the payoff of demonizing others is to feel good about ourselves.

My American colleague James Forbes is a bit suspicious of American zeal against apartheid. We find it all too easy to condemn South African whites who are prepared to exterminate the entire black population of South Africa, if necessary, in order to preserve their way of life. Yet we Americans are prepared to destroy the entire habitable planet in order to protect what we have!

Self-righteousness, however gross and counter-productive, is merely Satan's opening move. There is a far more subtle and insidious temptation, hard to identify even when we know that it exists. Thomas Merton named it the temptation to transform persons and social structures *from the outside.*[45] The danger here is that we assert our own individual conscience against the evil of the state. Jim Douglass explains:

> Protesting against something for which we ourselves are profoundly responsible is a futile exercise in hypocrisy. The evil of nuclear war is not external to us, so that it can be isolated in the state or in the Nuclear Train loaded with hydrogen bombs. The nature of the evil lies in our cooperation with it. What Merton is suggesting is that as we cease cooperating in one way with that evil, our well-hidden tendency is to begin cooperating with it more intensely and blindly in another way, defining evil in a way external to us which deepens and hardens its actual presence in ourselves.[46]

Whites who protest against the evils of the apartheid system are surely aware of the privileges with which that system endows them in the very act of resisting it. They are less likely to be arrested than blacks; if detained, far less likely to be tortured; will be treated with something far more resembling respect; will be released much sooner on average; will have powerful advocates on the outside clamoring for their release; and can raise bail and legal defense funds more easily. They also surely bear a crushing shame for having done so little previously to identify with the cause of black liberation. Worst of all, they have actually profited from apartheid. Their maids, their relative affluence, their fine homes, paved streets, sewage services, the unquestioning deference they still are paid by many blacks, their ability to petition government for their rights—all these things are genetically their solely by virture of being born white in a racist society, and they remain largely intact even when a white identifies completely with the black struggle. There is a complicity which is not willful but structural, and even our repentance cannot remove it.

Blacks also must acknowledge the extent to which they have cooperated with evil. Massive refusal by even half the black population in the early 1950s when the pass laws were consolidated would have arrested apartheid in its tracks. Why was it not forthcoming? The very appeal of a black separatist group like the Azanian People's Organization (AZAPO) indicates that apartheid has triumphed in the minds even of some of its opponents.

The roots of violence lie within us even more deeply still. There is in each of us a vigilante that would kill to retain its position of privilege, however meager. There is a security officer that would love to torture those who have wronged us. There is an informer who would betray friends and even family to save its skin. The news often evokes these elements. A friend blurted out on reading a particularly depressing headline, "I wish someone would just strangle him!" I knew better, but I felt the same way.

Every outer evil inevitably attracts from our own depths parts of ourselves that resemble it. To engage evil is therefore a spiritual act, because it will require of us the rare courage to face our own most ancient and intractable evils within. It means abandoning one of the greatest and oldest lies: that the world is made up of good people and bad people. There is a double movement of psychic energy. We identify someone else as evil and unconsciously project our own evil onto that person. But the person or system that we call enemy also evokes the evil within, like a piano string set vibrating by a piercing scream. This two-way traffic of projection and introjection, if not halted, eventually becomes a form of mimesis, where each party begins to imitate the other.

What is so very painful in the spiritual discipline required to face this inner darkness is that some of it may not be redeemable. I would like to become nonviolent from the heart, but there is a killer, a torturer, a coward, and a dictator in me that would like to keep me in psychic detention forever. Call it Satan, the shadow, the dark side of God, whatever, it is a brute fact documented down through the history of the human race. Something there is in me that does not want to be redeemed, or see others freed as well. I believe this fact is universal. Christian theology calls it the fall or original sin. Judaism knows it as the evil impulse. Even recognizing that this aspect is in me does not free me of its power. I must bring a great deal of consciousness and forgiving love to bear on these parts of me in order to limit their damage. I must continually offer them up to God for whatever healing and transformation is possible. People who engage in nonviolent protest without at least some awareness of this cesspool of violence within them can actually jeopardize the lives of their compatriots. In a protest against the bomb, they themselves become the bomb, and explode.

It is hard enough getting people to engage in Jesus' way of resistance to evil. Then we tell them they have to go through an arduous spiritual discipline to neutralize the oppressor within! As Shelley Douglass puts it, we do not want to have to change our lives to bring about justice. The hardest moment comes when our own internal oppressor meets the outside reality that it supports. It is not out there, but in me, that the oppressor must die.[47]

For most people this may be asking too much. They prefer the heady, extroverted phase of action. But Jesus' way has built into it an uncanny solution. It lands many of its practitioners in jail. That is where Paul did much of his meditating, thinking, and writing, and Gandhi and King as well. The quotation just cited by Jim Douglass, and the earlier one from King, were both written in jail. Beyers Naude says that the best thing that ever happened to him was his banning. Strange, wry providence, that prison should have been, for so many we spoke to in South Africa, not the unfortunate price of protest, but the gracious, fiery crucible which, as one black labor organizer told us, "killed my fear and made me all the more determined to struggle for liberation, to death if necessary"—not said with bravado, but with a quiet, serene smile.

Five: Not a Law but a Gift

Jesus' Third Way is not a law but a gift. It establishes us in freedom, not necessity. It is not something we are required to do, but enabled to do. It is a "Thou mayest," not a "Thou must." It is not something we do in order to secure our own righteousness before God. It is rather something that we are made capable of when we know that the power of God is greater than the powers of death.

Much as I fantasize about violence toward my enemies, I cannot conceive of actually killing them. Yet even if I am committed to nonviolence, I may find myself in a situation where I am not able to find a creative, third way, and must choose between the lesser of two violences, two guilts. Even then, however, it is not a question of justifying the violence. I simply must, as Bonhoeffer did, take on myself the guilt and cast myself on the mercy of God.[48] But in a situation of extreme oppression, it is far better that we act violently than let our fear of sin and guilt paralyze us into no act at all. I cannot even be sure that my nonviolent acts are just, or right, or willed by God.

Nor can we condemn those who in desperation resort to counter-violence against the massive violence of an unjust order. We should not strike a neutral pose, says John Swomley, but side with the oppressed, even if they follow the bad example of their oppressors in resorting to violence. "I wanted the oppressed Hungarians to gain their freedom from the Soviet Union in 1956," he writes, "even though they used violence."[49] Violence is not an absolute evil to be avoided at all costs. It is not even the main problem, but only the presenting symptom of an unjust society. And peace is not the highest good; it is rather the outcome of a just social order.

The Nicaraguan revolution has often been cited as an example where violence "worked," as it indeed did. But violent revolt there was not inevitable. Miguel D'Escoto, Nicaragua's foreign minister and a Roman Catholic priest, tells why.

Eight years before the insurrection, after the earthquake, I talked to the archbishop. And I said, "Archbishop, don't you see how this is going to explode?" To me it seemed inevitable that sooner or later in spite of the great patience of our people—everything human is limited—that patience would run out. I said, "Bishop, it is going to be terrible, there will be so many dead people, so much destruction and death. Why don't we go into the streets? You lead us, armed with the rosary in our hands and prayers on our lips and chants and songs in repudiation for what has been done to our people. The worst that can happen to us is the best, to share with Christ the cross if they shoot us.

"If they do shoot us, there will be a consciousness aroused internationally. And maybe the people in the United States will be alerted and will pressure their government so that it won't support Somoza, and then maybe we can be freed without the destruction that I see ahead."

And the archbishop said, "No Miguel, you tend to be a little bit idealistic, and this destruction is not going to happen." And then when it did happen, the church insisted on nonviolence.

To be very frank with you, I don't think that violence is Christian. Some may say that this is a reactionary position. But I think that the very essence of Christianity is the cross. It is through the cross that we will change.

I have come to believe that creative nonviolence has to be a constitutive element of evangelization and of the proclamation of the gospel. But in Nicaragua nonviolence was never included in the process of evangelization.

The cancer of oppression and injustice and crime and exploitation was allowed to grow, and finally the people had to fight with the means available to them, the only means that people have found from of old: armed struggle. Then the church arrogantly said violence was bad, nonviolence was the correct way.

I don't believe that nonviolence is something you can arrive at rationally. We can develop it as a spirituality and can obtain the grace necessary to practice it, but not as a result of reason. Not that it is anti-reason, but that it is not natural. The natural thing to do when somebody hits you is to hit them back.

We are called upon to be supernatural. We reach that way of being, not as a result of nature, but of prayer. But that spirituality and prayer and work with people's consciences has never been done. We have no right to hope to harvest what we have not sown.[50]

The counter-violence of the oppressed may even in the mystery of God's wrath be something which God is able to employ. Just as God used Assyrian military conquest as the rod to punish Israel for its apostasy (Isa. 10:5), so black violence has awakened some people to the severity of black discontent. And by preoccupying the security forces, that violence may even have provided an opening, a space, for the successful nonviolent actions in the past two years, which otherwise might have been crushed. So while I do not believe that Christians have a vocation for violence, and should actively oppose its use, we are also not permitted to sit in judgment over those who resort to violence. God can take care of that.

Six: The Way of the Cross

Jesus' Third Way is the way of the cross. The cross was not just Jesus' identification with the victims of oppression; it was, as Rob Robertson remarks, also his way of dealing with these evils. It was not because he was a failed insurrectionist that Jesus died as he did, but because he preferred to suffer injustice and violence rather than be their cause.[51] Following the Philippines' successful nonviolent revolution, Bishop Francisco Claver, SJ wrote, "We choose nonviolence not merely as a strategy for the attaining of the ends of justice, casting it aside if it does not work. We choose it as an end in itself...because we believe it is the way Christ himself struggled for justice."[52]

The cross means that death is not the greatest evil one can suffer. It means that I am free to act faithfully without undo regard for the outcome. God can bring out of voluntarily assumed suffering the precious seeds of a new reality. I cannot really be open to the call of God in a situation of oppression if the one thing I have excluded as an option is my own suffering and death.

Jesus' Third Way is not natural. We have not been prepared for it through millions of years of conditioning for flight or fight responses. We do not come to these things by virtue of a sunny disposition but by conversion, discipline, practice, imagination, and risk. Nonviolent training needs to become a regular and repetitive component of every change-oriented group's life; it is not a last minute strategy that can be donned at will like an asbestos suit.

The cross also means not necessarily winning. The Principalities and Powers are so colossal, entrenched and determined that the odds for their overthrow or repentance are minuscule, whatever means we use. It is precisely because the outcome is in question, however, that we need to choose a way of living that already is a living of the outcome we desire. The Reign of God is already in the process of arriving when we choose means consistent with its arrival. So for Gandhi the question, after one, two, three decades of struggle, was never: Shall we abandon *satyagraha* for violence? That would have been like asking, Shall I give up my integrity for the sake of the truth?

There is a horrible, yet I am afraid, absolutely accurate vision in Revelation 6:9–11, at the opening of the fifth seal:

> When he opened the fifth seal, I saw under the altar the souls of those who had been slain for the word of God and for the witness they had borne; they cried out with a loud voice, "O Sovereign Lord, holy and true, how long before thou wilt judge and avenge our blood on those who dwell upon the earth?" Then they were each given a white robe and told to rest a little longer, until the number of their fellow servants and their brethren should be complete, who were to be killed as they themselves had been.

No one believes South Africa can be transformed without violence. Jesus' Third Way is certainly no way of avoiding it. On the contrary, Jesus' way deliberately evokes the violence of an oppressive system, using its momentum to throw it. As Charles Williams remarked, if the energy of evil is to be deflected or transformed, something or someone must suffer its impact. The only question is, What level of suffering will be necessary? The vision in Revelation is a sober reminder that Jesus' way will inevitably result in casualties. Certainly the casualties may be fewer by a huge margin than in a hot war, but they will be painful to bear nonetheless. The weight of each death, like a fallen snowflake, adds to the accumulated mass, until the branch snaps.

The cross requires courage. During the vigilante torching of Crossroads/KTC, June 9–11, 1986, John Freeth, an Anglican priest, moved back and forth under fire between the vigilantes and their victims, helping the wounded, comforting the dying, trying to get the police to stop the carnage. He noticed that many of the black vigilantes looked down or away when he encountered them, as if they felt ashamed for what they were doing. It occurred to him that if he could only find twenty-five clergy willing to make a human chain between the opposing black factions, that it would give those vigilantes who had been recruited against their wishes a face-saving way to back off. The moral force of the act and the public exposure it involved would make it hard for the instigators to press the attack. It also would unmask police support for the attacking vigilantes and give the lie to their bogus claims that they were attempting to prevent violence.

A capital idea, I said (by phone from the United States). Can you find twenty-five? "Twenty-five?" he laughed. "So far I've had difficulty finding two and a half! Most think I'm a bit potty." Did he just not know whom to call? Or did they know so little of the history of nonviolent interventions that this tested and often successful tactic appeared to them bizarre? Or was it—I hesitate to put it so baldly, but someone must—a case of sheer cowardice?

Or was it a bit of all three, abetted by an even more significant factor: the lack of a structure for summoning and empowering people to transcend their perfectly natural and prudent fear? Prior to undergoing nonviolence training in Selma in 1965 I was shaking in my socks. But fear is remarkably responsive to the Holy Spirit. It need not remain in our path, blocking our obedience; we can put it behind us, where it continues to whimper but no longer determines our deeds.

Daniel Berrigan observes that most people find it more sane to contemplate nuclear suicide than civil disobedience. Millions march off willingly to wars, fortified by blind trust in chance: the unexpressed hope that it will be their buddies who get it, not they themselves, and that they will kill the enemy, not be killed. It takes far more courage to walk into a situation voluntarily, knowing that suffering is inevitable, choosing to draw the poison of that violence with one's own body rather than perpetuating the downward spiral of hate. But that is what we celebrate in every Eucharist as Jesus' way. Will it not be ours as well?

Visions
of
the
Future

Chapter Five

Scenario-sketching has become the number one growth industry in South Africa. The best scenario I came across was from Stephen Mulholland, a South African journalist, who tells foreign audiences that the answer to every question about what will happen in South Africa is Yes.

Can there be a military coup? Yes.
Can there be a bloodbath? Yes.
Can there be a white right-wing takeover? Yes.
Can there be a black Marxist takeover? Yes.
Can there be peaceful evolution? Yes.
Can there be more of the same, repression and reform? Yes.
What about a federal system? Yes.
Can there be economic collapse? Yes.
What about Rhodesian style hothouse economic growth? Yes.
Do you want to emigrate? Yes.
Do you want to stay there? Yes.[53]

What Mulholland's witty response means is that the future is still open. Not wide. Perhaps only barely.

But catastrophe has not yet become South Africa's inevitable fate. It is highly probable but not certain. The churches of South Africa can still help determine that future. Visions have a way of creating new possibilities. Let me share something of the vision that I believe I glimpse as a conceivable alternative to your gathering apocalypse.

The first vision has to do with involving Christians and their churches more actively in the struggle for liberation. I would commend something on the order of Martin Luther King, Jr.'s Southern Christian Leadership Conference (SCLC). This loose-knit organization drew together black clergy who were committed to nonviolent direct action, had taken nonviolence training, and were willing to put their bodies on the line. I believe something like that is needed in South Africa, but organized interracially. One white pastor shared how isolated he was in the East Rand, how conservative his parishoners were, and how difficult it was for him to do anything by himself. He suddenly thought of the same tactic used so successfully in Selma, Alabama, the great turning point of the civil rights struggle. When a crisis occurs, why not have clergy from all over the area or even the country converge on that town en masse, lending visibility and protection to those who are being oppressed? This would concentrate personnel who are now so widely scattered, prevent local leaders from being so easily isolated and picked off, give moral support to those who struggle in obscurity, and provide moral legitimation to their cause. Funds could be raised locally and internationally to facilitate travel and communication.

I ran this idea by Beyers Naude. "Yes, we tried that several times in the past," he said, "but we simply could not find enough clergy willing to come." I would have thought that the trauma of the past two years would have radicalized a significant number of clergy, but John Freeth's experience mentioned earlier warns otherwise. I am not persuaded that cowardice is the chief cause, however. What is needed, it seems to me, is a structure capable of galvanizing a lightning response by precommitted clergy who have already settled in advance the key questions about tactics, rationale, and readiness to risk.

And why limit it to clergy? Their great advantage is their visible identity: the collar. Why not have another symbol for laity, something similar to Black Sash, that enables them to join on a basis of complete parity and opens the movement to a wider base of support?

As Naude pointed out to me, such a course of action would create a critical need for nonviolence training. Participants would need theological and political clarity about the centrality of this teaching to Christian faith in order to sustain themselves under the tremendous pressures to which they would be subjected. In the United States, for example, there is a network of some 80,000 people who have pledged in advance that if significant military escalation by the United States takes place in Central America, they will commit acts of civil disobedience or engage in nonviolent demonstrations. Training in nonviolence is a condition of this pledge.

One key to the success of the nonviolent victory in the Philippines was the degree of participation by the churches' top leadership in nonviolence training. A year and a half before Marcos was toppled from power, Jean and Hildegard Goss-Mayr of the

International Fellowship of Reconciliation were invited by Filipino Christians to come to the Philippines to hold seminars on the Gospel and active nonviolence. These seminars lasted six weeks and included one with thirty Roman Catholic bishops. Richard Deats, also with the Fellowship of Reconciliation, followed with three weeks of training, primarily for Protestants. Out of these seminars a group of Filipinos founded AKKAPKA ("Action for Peace and Justice"). Within the year AKKAPKA, under the leadership of Fr. Jose Blanco and Tess Ramiro, held forty nonviolence seminars in thirty provinces, with the cooperation of many Filipino bishops, clergy, nuns, and lay leaders. At strategy sessions, which regularly included Cory Aquino and Cardinal Sin, various scenarios for protecting against election fraud were discussed. When the crisis came, AKKAPKA and other organizations had trained half a million poll watchers who were prepared to give their lives to prevent falsification of ballots.

Later, when key military leaders defected to a "rebel" army base, Cardinal Sin went to three orders of contemplative nuns and told them, "We are now in battle. Prostrate yourselves, pray and fast. You are the powerhouse of God and central to the battle. Fast until death if necessary." Then, over the Catholic radio, Cardinal Sin called upon the people to place their unarmed bodies between the defectors and the government troops. There were only a few in the beginning, but soon hundreds of thousands of people made a human wall around the base, tying yellow ribbons on the gun barrels of tanks and offering soldiers gifts of food, candies, and garlands of flowers. President Marcos ordered the tanks to attack. Their commanders refused to proceed when nuns and priests sat in front of their tracks. Pilots, ordered to bomb the rebel base with its human cordon, refused and defected to a nearby United States military base.[54]

There were other factors in the success of nonviolence in the Philippines. Bishop Francisco Claver, SJ was tireless in holding up the relation of nonviolence to the Gospel year after year. Ninoy Aquino converted to nonviolence in prison where he studied violent, third world revolutions and came in the end to feel that Gandhi, rather than Mao and others, was his mentor. He returned from exile armed only with "faith and determination." After he was murdered, his wife Cory took up his fallen banner. Above all, the Filipino people have been willing to hold fast to a nonviolent style of resistance.

I am not for a moment suggesting that the situations of the Philippines and South Africa are similar. But every struggle has its lessons. In the Philippines, a number of advocates of Jesus' Third Way (Muriel Lester, E. Stanley Jones, Toyohiko Kagawa, John Nevin Sayre, Frank Laubach, Glenn Smiley, John Swomley and Richard Deats) planted seeds quietly over several decades. Then at the height of the crisis under Marcos' rule, following the death of Ninoy Aquino, Filipinos developed a dynamic, uniquely indigenous nonviolent mass movement that successfully overthrew a powerful dictatorial regime.

Many people in South Africa have a foreshortened sense of time, as if it were now too late for nonviolence training, reflection, or deeds. One theologian brushed aside discussion of nonviolence with the comment that "people subjected to violence don't philosophize about it." That is certainly true if the church fails to lift their struggles to the level of reflection. But the key contribution of liberation theology is precisely its understanding of *praxis*: theological reflection on action. If "they don't philosophize," is it because they have no need for it, or because our Bible studies, sermons and lectures are failing to address the issues?

The conflict in South Africa has simmered along for decades. Periodically it reaches a boil. Apart from the successful use of brute force to crush all dissent, however, I see little likelihood of a speedy resolution. It is not too late to begin a massive program of training in nonviolence to supplement, inform, and bring much-needed discipline to the welter of nonviolent actions already going on. It is certainly not too late to begin involving more and more white Christians in such activities. More fundamentally still, we must assert as a matter of faith that it is never too late to begin following the Third Way of Jesus.

The debate about violence versus nonviolence is simply no longer fruitful. Nonviolent acts of civil disobedience, protest and confrontation are, for most people, the only effective actions possible. And let no one say, "But the government will never allow it." The government does not allow violence either. The oppressed and their allies simply are no longer asking what the government allows. They are fostering what Jonathan Schell calls "an epidemic of freedom in a closed society"[55] by ignoring official permissions and living "as if" the new society were at hand. Increased governmental controls will not be the occasion for abandoning nonviolence. They will simply make it costlier.

The first draft of this book was completed before the second National Emergency of June, 1986. In an attempt to discover what effect the emergency was having, we called Sheena Duncan, past president of Black Sash. She said that the emergency had created a qualitatively new situation, with restrictions so complete and penalties so exorbitant that nonviolent actions had come to a complete halt. In an eloquent tribute to the power of nonviolence, the government had decided, in effect, to treat nonviolence as the equivalent of violence. Merely to make a statement that calls for an end to conscription, to engage in any form of demonstration, to criticize the government or any of its officers, or to urge support of boycotts, has become sedition punishable by ten years in prison and/or a 20,000 Rand fine. Our voices must have betrayed the impact of this devastating news. "Don't be discouraged," she reassured us, "it's only been two weeks. Nobody is sitting down and saying we can't go on. We're just trying to figure out what we can do next."

It is not unusual in a protracted struggle to experience bewilderment and even despair after each new measure taken by the Powers to crush rising opposition. That experience is not only characteristic, it is a necessary precondition of creative response. Creativity is always the improbable grasped out of the teeth of despair. The allure of violence at such times is understandable. It does not require the same degree of imagination and invention.

Our time has witnessed the emergence of a new historical phenomenon: the National Security State, a colossus of surveillance and repressive might made virtually impregnable as a result of the wizardry of military and electronic technology. Such a colossus should deprive us of all hope. But the paradoxical consequence is just the opposite. Since armed resistance is largely futile, people have taken recourse in nonviolent means. Nonviolence has even become the preferred method of people who have never contemplated absolute pacifism. Because anti-apartheid leaders are arrested almost as soon as they emerge, resistance groups have innovated non-hierarchical and democratic organizational forms. Means and ends coalesce as people create for themselves social instruments for change that already embody the better life they seek ahead. For this reason it seems to me that those of you who have held back from throwing the full weight of your moral authority into a nonviolent mode of struggle need do so no longer. The question is not pacifism, but a more effective, united struggle for goals shared by all. In the SCLC-type organization envisioned here, there would not even be the need for people to reach theoretical agreement on nonviolence as a total philosophy, as long as they were agreed that in specific campaigns they would remain nonviolent.

Many people have not aspired to Jesus' Third Way because it has been presented to them as absolute pacifism, a life-commitment to nonviolence in principle, with no exceptions. They are neither sure that they can hold fast to its principles in every situation nor that they have the saintliness to overcome their own inner violence. Perhaps a more traditional Christian approach would make more sense. We know that nonviolence is the New Testament pattern. We can commit ourselves to following Jesus' way as best we can. We know we are weak and will probably fail. But we also know that God loves and forgives us and sets us back on our feet after every failure and defeat.

Seen in this light, Jesus' Third Way is not an insuperable counsel to perfection attainable only by the few. It is simply the right way to live, and can be pursued by the many. The more who attempt it, the more mutual support there will be in following it.

Blacks are already up to their ears in nonviolent direct actions, much as they may dislike the expression. It is the white community that needs to be mobilized. Whites have no right to preach nonviolence to blacks; they only have a right to act it. Some blacks may object to being shielded by whites occasionally, or subjected to white liberal paternalism with its unbelievable ignorance of black reality. We can only beg them to regard the whole thing as remedial education for whites.

Blacks are not looking for whites to solve their problems. They know that the shape of the future has passed into their hands. But they do need to know that there are white Christians who identify with their cause to the point of dying if necessary. And they can use all the allies they can get. There is some evidence, for example, that the presence of white clergy at black funerals reduces police provocations and violence.

There is a great deal more white churches can do on their own, even given congregational resistance to change. There are churches that have decided to integrate their preschool programs, in defiance of the law. There are churches giving genuine support to their young people in the End Conscription Campaign. There are churches serving interracial meals, exchanging pastors from white and black churches, and even taking whole congregations to visit each others' churches. There are university Christian groups that are posting on bulletin boards the names of local stores that refuse to serve all races and urging people not to patronize them.

Many dismiss this as too little, too late. It may be. It is also something else: the church edging cautiously toward becoming an alternative society within the shell of the old. At this historical juncture every act of interracial contact and understanding is a blow against apartheid. All such acts are important, even if they are not enough.

But so much more needs to be done! South African Christians can, in this historical moment, make a contribution that will be honored for all eternity. But it will have to be a response of heroic proportions. You are living through a time when, as Christopher Frye put it, "wrong comes up to face us everywhere, never to leave us till we take the longest stride of soul man ever took. Affairs are now soul-sized."[56] How fortunate you are to have as your prophetic leaders some of the great figures of our epoch and, as theologians, some as able as any in the world.

The future is no cause for optimism. Black vigilantes are destroying community solidarity, murdering anti-apartheid leaders and torching entire locations. A right-wing coup with heightened repression and Nazi-like values seems almost an inevitability that will simply have to be endured. (Some people think that coup has already taken place.) Frustration at the delay of liberation in townships can turn inward, like gangrene, and eat the heart out of the courageous opposition. International sanctions may increase hunger, malnutrition, and unemployment. The nightmarish list could go on and on.

All that, and worse, is quite likely. What people forget though, and what Mulholland left off his list, is what Peter Storey, a former president of the Methodist Church in Southern Africa, calls the X-factor: the unforeseen, unexpected, surprise ending. Almost no historical event is ever fully predictable, most especially those born of such fantastic forces as are in play in South Africa today. No one could have predicted the defection of the defense minister and the military chief of staff in the Philippines. No one could have dared dream that civilians would succeed in nonviolently stopping planes and tanks by surrounding the rebel base. ("This is something new," exclaimed one of the defectors, Colonel Alimonte. "Soldiers are supposed to protect the civilians. In this particular case, you have civilians protecting the soldiers."[57])

In South Africa we found the greatest hope among blacks. In the past several years they have, for the first time, experienced some successes. "I've never seen hope displayed as it is today," said one black community organizer. "Whenever people go out they know some will die, but it doesn't stop them."

Many whites we spoke with felt only despair. Significantly, those who did not were, in every case, actively related to the black community. Part of the drama going on in South Africa then is the possible purification of white Christianity (and that includes the "white" elements still dominant in the black churches) in the furnace of the black liberation struggle. The English-speaking churches, most of them eighty percent black, can scarcely avoid this baptism by fire. And who knows; perhaps the greatest surprises of all will come from repentant white Dutch Reformed Christians.

Those are a few glimpses of an alternative vision for the churches. But what of the nation? According to Scripture, every nation has an angel which represents the personality and the divine calling of its people. What is the vocation of South Africa's "angel"?[58] What vision can we hold before us of its possible future in order to counter the self-fulfilling prophecies of doom? A white pastor, who spends his day-off counselling blacks suffering from post-detainment trauma, shared his dream of:

> ...a nation that could produce a culture as rich as any the world has ever seen. Blacks could enrich whites with their sense of community, their music, their joy. Whites have great skills and expertise to contribute. Together we could create a beautiful country, a genuinely interracial, finally nonracial society, one person one vote. That's what I work for every day. I would like to be governed by blacks, and could even put up with black consciousness for awhile in order to redress the imbalance.

That is not what he expects to happen. But hope is never based on current evidence, or it could scarcely exist. As W. H. Auden put it so simply,

> Nothing can save us that is possible.
> We who must die demand a miracle.[59]

Ah, Angel of South Africa, I listened closely for your voice, drowned out by the grating and clash of gigantic social forces and the glum dirge of fear and despair. You were hard to hear. Did I imagine it, or did you tell me that you see a new system of government emerging, unlike any the world has known; that you see wealth gradually (far too gradually) redistributed, improving the lot of the poor; that you see African culture in cross-fertilization with Western culture, producing a stupendous outpouring of drama, literature, religious vitality, and above all, music, in a context of continuous conflict and high- to low-level violence, which over ten to fifty years will gradually abate as South Africa finally works out a more just way of being?

That at least is a vision worth working for. But we cannot be assured that it is the future. The X-factor is too great. That X-factor now rests to a high degree squarely in the hands of the churches. We need to play our games of prognostication, but this is a script whose outcome will keep us in suspense all along the way. Will you be among those who, by your courageous fidelity to Jesus' Third Way, help to write that script in the days ahead?

Footnotes

1. Ronald J. Sider and Richard K. Taylor, *Nuclear Holocaust and Christian Hope* (Downers Grove, Ill.: Intervarsity Press, 1982), 250–51.

2. Gene Sharp, *The Politics of Nonviolent Action* (Boston: Porter Sargent, 1973), 117–434. See also Sider and Taylor, pp. 236–87.

3. "Resistance to evil by peaceful means" is an accurate rendition of *satyagraha*, but it is confusing, since the means King and Gandhi chose often deliberately provoked conflict and shattered a bogus "peace" masking systemic or legalized violence. The Brazilians have found a nice phrase in *firmeza permanente*, "relentless firmness," which is an excellent translation for the New Testament virtue of *hupomonē*. Luke 21:12–19, for example, predicts that the faithful "will be brought before synagogues and put in prison; you will be haled before kings and governors for your allegiance to me...Even your parents and brothers, your relations and friends, will betray you. Some of you will be put to death...By *standing firm* (*hupomonē*) you will win true life for yourselves" (NEB). The term connotes "endurance, obstinacy, power to sustain blows, fortitude, perseverance, steadfastness"—relentless firmness quite ably catches the meaning. One definition of *satyagraha* also coincides with *hupomonē*: "power which comes through a tenacious devotion to the ultimate reality" (William Robert Miller,

Nonviolence [New York: Schocken Books, 1972], 28). This quality of absolute intransigence before the attempts by political authorities to crush resistance is identified as an indispensable characteristic of Christian existence in the Book of Revelation (1:9; 2:2, 3, 19; 3:10; 13:10; 14:12). Its anemic rendition as "patient endurance" in the RSV is itself a political act.

4. In April, 1986, the South African magazine *Praxis* ran a poem by Cecil Rajendra that tells the heart-rending story of a man who decides to kill his starving family and himself rather than suffer any longer. At the end the poet asks the reader, "Do you still believe in non-violence?" Rajendra completely identifies nonviolence with submission and the acceptance of injustice.

5. *The Kairos Document: Challenge to the Church* (Braamfontein: The Kairos Theologians, 1985). This manifesto arose from the grassroots as a challenge to the churches to resist apartheid. The distinction the authors have made between "State Theology," "Church Theology," and "Prophetic Theology" is a permanent contribution to theological thought.

6. Blood River marked an overwhelming victory over Zulus in 1838 in which not a single Afrikaner life was lost. The Great Trek was an "exodus" out of British domination in the Cape into the "promised land" of the interior. Of these and like events Prime Minister D. S. Malan said, "Our history is the greatest masterpiece of the centuries. We hold this nationhood as our due for it was given us by the Architect of the universe. [His] aim was the formation of a new nation among the nations of the world....The last hundred years have witnessed a miracle behind which must lie a divine plan. Indeed the history of the Afrikaner reveals a will and a determination which makes one feel that Afrikanerdom is not the work of man but the creation of God." (Cited by Charles Villa-Vicencio, *The Theology of Apartheid* (Capetown: Methodist Publishing House, n.d.), 19.

7. *The Kairos Document.*

8. Cited by John W. DeGruchy, *Bonhoeffer and South Africa* (Grand Rapids: Eerdmans, 1984), 98.

9. William Robert Miller, *Nonviolence*, 51.

10. Fr. Buti Tlhagale, "Christian Soldiers," *Leadership* 5/1 (1986): 45–49.

11. *Anthistēmi* is the Greek word most frequently used in the Septuagint to translate the Hebrew *qum* and often carries the sense of "to rise up" against someone in revolt or war (Gen. 4:8; Num. 16:2; Judg. 9:35, 43; 20:33; 2 Chron. 13:6; Ps. 94:16 [93:16 LXX]; Isa. 14:22; Amos 7:9; Obad. 1; Hab. 2:7. *Epanistēmi* is used synonymously: Deut. 19:11; 22:26; 33:11; Judg. 9:18; Job 20:27; 27:7; 30:12; Ps. 27:3; Isa. 31:2; Mic. 7:6. So also *katephistamai* (Acts 18:12—"made insurrection," KJV; "made a united attack," RSV) and *akatastasia* (Luke 21:9—"revolutions," JB; "insurrections," KJV, NEB). *Anthistēmi* is also used of armed, violent warfare in 3 Macc. 6:19; Rom. 13:2; and Eph. 6:13. Liddell/Scott define it as "to set against, especially in battle." We can be virtually assured that it is used in Matt. 5:39 in the sense of "to resist forcibly" because the Jesus tradition elsewhere cites Mic. 7:6—"For the son treats the father with contempt, the daughter rises up against her mother, the daughter-in-law against her mother-in-law; a man's enemies are the men of his own house" (see Matt. 10:34–36; Luke 12:53). And Jesus may have formulated the statement about debtors giving their clothing to creditors in contrast to Hab. 2:7, where the wealthy are threatened with visions of debtors suddenly rising up in bloody revolt. Both passages use a form of *qum*.

12. Matthew and Luke are utterly at odds on whether it is the outer garment (Luke) or the inner garment (Matthew) that is being taken. But the Jewish practice of giving the outer

garment as collateral for a loan makes it clear that Luke is correct.

13. *Babylonian Talmud, Baba Kamma* 92b.

14. *Weekly Mail*, April 25 to May 1, 1986, 5.

15. Gerd Theissen, *Biblical Faith; An Evolutionary Approach* (Philadelphia: Fortress Press, 1985), 122.

16. *Essays on Nonviolence*, ed. by Thérèse de Coninck (Nyack, NY: Fellowship of Reconciliation, n.d.), 38.

17. Jos., *War* 2.172–74; *Ant.* 18.55–59. Despite the similarity to a wolf's baring his throat to show he is overmastered, the two acts are polar opposites. The wolf is surrendering; these Jews were being defiant. The wolf seeks to save its life; these Jews were prepared to die for their faith. The Jews later tried the same tactic against the Emperor Gaius (Caligula), and again prevailed, aided by the providential death of the emperor (*Ant.* 18.257–309).

18. William Robert Miller, *Nonviolence*, 252.

19. "An Interview with Adolfo Peréz Esquivel," *Fellowship* 51(July/August): 1985, 10.

20. Saul Alinsky, *Rules for Radicals* (New York: Random House, 1971).

21. Gandhi, *The Science of Satyagraha*, ed. by Anand T. Hingorani (Bombay: Bharatiya Vidya Bhanan, 1970), 67.

22. Conversations with Doug Johnson and Elaine Lamy of INFACT.

23. "Prophets in Steeltown," *Christian Century*, May 8, 1985, 460–62.

24. Gandhi consistently turned away those who were fearful of taking up arms or felt themselves incapable of violent resistance. "Nonviolence cannot be taught to a person who fears to die and has no power of resistance." "He who has not overcome fear cannot practice *ahimsa* [the resolve not to hurt a living being] to perfection." "At every meeting I repeated the warning that unless they felt that in non-violence they had come into possession of a force infinitely superior to the one they had and in the use of which they were adept, they should have nothing to do with non-violence and resume the arms they had possessed before" (cited by Joan V. Bondurant, *Conquest of Violence* [Princeton: Princeton University Press, 1958], 28–29, 139).

25. *Weekly Mail*, April 18 to April 24, 1986, 4.

26. *Weekly Mail*, May 2 to May 8, 1986, 4.

27. I wonder if perhaps something of the same romanticism clouds theological discussion of Bonhoeffer's involvement in the death plot against Hitler. Had it succeeded, would it have been any more successful than the assassination of Verwoerd in 1966? When Hitler finally committed suicide, one of his generals simply assumed power and continued the war. Hitler rode to power on the back of an entire ethos, party structure, military, and ideology. He was merely the catalyst for an invisible but palpable spirituality that had possessed the German nation. Assassination would also have justified a new version of the "stabbed in the back" myth that fueled German discontent after World War I. It would have made Hitler a martyr. Even if it had shortened the war, it would have

spared Germany the trauma of warfare on its own soil, an experience which German Bishop Hans Lilje believed necessary in order to rid the German soul of some of its militaristic tendencies.

28. John W. Swomley, Jr., *Liberation Ethics* (New York: Macmillan, 1972), 172. On Solidarity, see the exceptional article by Jonathan Schell in the February 3, 1986 *New Yorker*, "Reflections: A Better Today," 47–67.

29. Data from Rob Robertson, "Response to the Kairos Document," 30 October, 1985.

30. Swomley, *Liberation Ethics*, 172.

31. *The Weekly Mail*, May 23 to 29, 1986, 4. For data on the South African struggle generally, I have drawn on Leo Kuper, *Passive Resistance in South Africa* (New Haven: Yale University Press, 1957), and Mary Benson, *South Africa. The Struggle for a Birthright* (Middlesex: Penguin Books, 1966).

32. Breyten Breytenbach, *The True Confessions of an Albino Terrorist* (Emmarentia: Taurus, 1984), 70–71.

33. Miles D. Wolpin, *Militarism and Social Revolution in the Third World* (Totowa, N.J.: Allanheld, Osmun and Co., 1981), 3.

34. Martin Luther King, Jr., sermon delivered at Dexter Ave. Baptist Church in Montgomery, Alabama at Christmas, 1957, written in the Montgomery jail during the bus boycott. Reprinted in the A. J. Muste Essay Series, number 1 (New York: A. J. Muste Memorial Institute, 339 Lafayette St., New York, NY 10012).

35. John Stoner, letter presented to the Kirkridge gathering of peace leaders, 1984.

36. Thomas Merton, *Conjectures of a Guilty Bystander* (Garden City, NY: Doubleday & Co., Inc., 1966), 56.

37. *New York Times*, Sunday, August 3, 1986.

38. Bondurant, *Conquest of Violence*, 50.

39. Narayan Desai, letter to Françoise Pottier, January 27, 1986, courtesy of Richard Deats.

40. Milan Machovec, *A Marxist Looks at Jesus* (Philadelphia: Fortress Press, 1976), 108–109. In this regard, M. Scott Peck's otherwise remarkable book, *People of the Lie* (New York: Simon and Schuster, 1983), is flawed by his refusal to see the parents of his patients as themselves the victims of parents who were victims *ad infinitum*. As a consequence he demonizes people who also have a story that would evoke understanding and forgiveness if we only knew it. We are not contending against flesh and blood, but against the Powers: with the systems, structures, values, ideologies and role images that make people the witting or unwitting servants of the "father of lies." To put it bluntly, Jesus also died for the people of the lie, and all of us are such people.

41. Daniel Yergin, *Shattered Peace. The Origins of the Cold War and the National Security State* (Boston: Houghton Mifflin Co., 1977), 53.

42. Swomley, *Liberation Ethics*, 104.

43. Rob Robertson, "Response to the Kairos Document."

44. Allan Boesak, *Black and Reformed* (Johannesburg: Skotaville Publishers, 1984), 59.

45. Thomas Merton, *Mystics and Zen Masters*, cited by

Jim Douglass in "Civil Disobedience as Prayer," *Ground Zero*, February/March, 1985.

46. Ibid.

47. Shelley Douglass, "Being Clear," *Ground Zero*, September/October, 1984.

48. "Before other men the man of free responsibility is justified by necessity; before himself he is acquitted by his conscience; but before God he hopes only for mercy" (Dietrich Bonhoeffer, *Ethics* [New York: Macmillan, 1963], 248).

49. John W. Swomley, Jr., "Response to Gordon Zahn," *Fellowship* 43 (1977): 8.

50. Miguel D'Escoto, "An Unfinished Canvas," *Sojourners*, March 1983, 17.

51. Rob Robertson, "Response to the Kairos Document."

52. "Nonviolence Wins the Philippines," Fellowship of Reconciliation leaflet, Box 271, Nyack, NY 10960.

53. Stephen Mulholland, "An Act of Faith," in *The South Africans. Visions of the Future* (Cape Town: *Leadership*, January, 1986), 32–34.

54. Richard Deats, "The Revolution That Didn't Just Happen," *Fellowship* 52 (July/August, 1986): 3–4; Peggy Rosenthal, "The Precarious Road," *Commonweal*, June 20, 1986, 364–67.

55. Schell, "Reflections," 57.

56. Christopher Frye, *A Sleep of Prisoners* (New York: Dramatists Play Service, 1953), 62.

57. "Nonviolence Wins the Philippines."

58. See my *Unmasking the Powers* (Philadelphia: Fortress Press, 1986), chapter 4, where I argue that the biblical image of the angel of the nation (Dan. 10) is symbolic of the spirituality of a nation, both its personality as a collective entity and its vocation as a creation of God. Even though this notion has been severely abused in Afrikaner theology, and requires correction and renovation, it remains an indispensable biblical category.

59. W. H. Auden, *For the Time Being*, in *The Collected Poetry of W.H. Auden* (New York: Random House, 1945), 411.

60. *Weekly Mail*, May 2 to May 8, 1986, 4.

The Fellowship of Reconciliation

The Fellowship of Reconciliation (FOR) is a religious, pacifist organization founded in England in 1914 and in the United States a year later. Today there are branches or affiliated movements of the International Fellowship of Reconciliation in more than thirty countries. Members include Christians, Jews, Buddhists, Hindus, Muslims and others who share a faith in the power of love and truth for resolving human conflict.

While it has always been vigorous in its opposition to war, the Fellowship has insisted equally that this effort must be based on a committment to achieving a just and peaceful world community, with full dignity and freedom for every human being.

In working out these objectives the FOR seeks the company of people of faith who will respond to conflict nonviolently, seeking reconciliation through compassionate action. The Fellowship encourages the integration of faith into the lives of individual members. At the same time it is a special role of the Fellowship to extend the boundaries of community and to affirm its diversity of religious traditions as it seeks the resolution of conflict by the united efforts of people of many faiths.

In the development of its program the FOR depends upon persons who seek to apply these principles to every area of life. FOR members:

Identify with those of every nation, race, sex and religion who are victims of injustice and exploitation, and seek to develop resources of active nonviolent intervention with which to help rescue them from such circumstances;

Work to abolish war and to create a community of concern transcending national boundaries and selfish interests; they refuse to participate personally in any war, or to give any sanction they can withhold from physical, moral, psychological or financial preparations for war;

Strive to build a social order that will utilize the resources of human ingenuity and wisdom for the benefit of all, and in which no individual or group will be exploited or oppressed for the profit or pleasure of others;

Advocate fair and compassionate methods of dealing with offenders against society; they also serve as advocates for victims of crime and their families who suffer loss and emotional anguish, recognizing that restitution and reconciliation can help to heal both victims and offenders;

Endeavor to show reverence for personality—in the home, in vocational relationships, in school and in the processes of education, in association with persons of other racial, creedal, or national backgrounds;

Seek to avoid bitterness and contention in dealing with controversy, and to maintain the spirit of self-giving love while engaged in the effort to achieve these purposes.

For further information contact:

Fellowship of Reconciliation
Box 271
Nyack, NY 10960 USA
(914) 358-4601

International Fellowship of Reconciliation
Hof van Sonoy, 1811 LD
Alkmaar, The Netherlands
072.123.014

Afterword

As I write, 3100 copies of this volume, under the title *Jesus' Third Way*, are slowly wending their way by a myriad of means to the clergy of the English-speaking churches of South Africa. We have no idea whether the authorities there are intercepting them or letting them through. We hope enough arrive to contribute at least to a discussion of violence and nonviolence in the South African setting. I am grateful to the Fellowship of Reconciliation for raising the necessary funds.

This new printing provides a chance for me to comment further on the issues this book addresses. Shortly after I had finished writing it, I bumped into a well-known Christian ethicist who has a long history of involvement with and concern for South Africa. I gave him a brief rundown of the conclusions I had reached on my visit to South Africa—that though the odds were maybe less than one-half of one percent of being successful, a concerted effort by the churches to engage in nonviolent struggle on behalf of the oppressed might have a decisive impact on the fate of the nation. I was not trying to tell the African National Congress what to do (though I clearly had my own preferences), but was trying to rouse that sleeping giant, the English-speaking churches, whose memberships are about eighty percent black, to effective and decisive nonviolent actions against apartheid. He smiled a tight, knowing smile and said with finality, "The South African situation will be resolved the way these things always are, by violence," and turned to converse with someone else.

In a variety of ways I have encountered the same response repeatedly from Americans. There is a curious preference for violence, not just because the injustices in South Africa are so horrible that people want them ended quickly, but because violence has become, for many less astute followers of "Christian realism," the preferred method for settling such matters. There is an ironic romanticism about violence among these "realists." It is evident the moment one begins to press them for details of precisely how they conceive carrying out a violent revolution.

I found the same phenomenon in South Africa where I spoke to many people who were convinced that counter-violence alone could answer the violence routinely practiced by the apartheid government. But I did not find a single person who would explore with me the precise means to wage a successful armed revolution.

I pointed out, for example, the vast difference between landlocked Zimbabwe (formerly Rhodesia), where arms had been smuggled across the borders from almost every side, and South Africa, with easily patrolled oceans on three sides and the Kalahari Desert on the fourth, leaving only the strips of border facing Angola and Mozambique for moving weapons into the country. And these strips are protected by mines, barbed wire, and the redoubtable South African Defense Forces, which do not hesitate to make incursions deep into bordering territories in search of guerrilla camps. The romanticists simply do not want to admit that no sizable amount of weapons will be smuggled into South Africa in the foreseeable future. After twenty-five years of guerrilla struggle within South Africa, only twenty-nine grenades were detonated in all of 1985![60] I see no possible way adequate arms could be supplied for a full-scale urban guerrilla war, much less for the massive resupplying efforts a hot war would require.

One South African white argued that the time has passed for whites to tell blacks what to do. If blacks have decided that armed resistance is the only remaining way (in fact, most have not), then it is the task of whites to supply them with weapons. I responded, "And did you?" This was a very courageous person who acted on his convictions. "Yes," he replied, after some hesitation. "How many?" He was reluctant to answer. "I got some." "How many?" I insisted. "A few." That is precisely the point. "A few" is not enough. We are talking about shiploads, planeloads, for twenty-two million unarmed blacks. "A few" weapons will not be enough, and there are very few whites willing to supply them.

One American graduate student simply pooh-poohed the difficulties I posed in getting arms. When people need weapons, he argued, they can always get them. I pressed him repeatedly, "How? Just tell me how." "The Russians," he suggested. But does anyone really think the Soviet Union wants to risk a serious confrontation in southern Africa by launching a major arms supply effort, one which to be effective at all would have to include air-drops from cargo planes within South Africa's extensive and heavily defended territory? If the situation continues to deteriorate, the United Nations could send a military force, backed by both the United States and the Soviet Union. A United Nations force is the only violent option that has much chance of liberating blacks, and its proponents need to recognize that it would probably involve the virtual genocide of the Afrikaner population in order to succeed.

Given that prospect, should we not at least encourage the churches to throw the full force of their moral authority on the side of ending apartheid? No longer through words only, should the churches not use their massive reservoir of untapped power to do militant nonviolent acts of civil disobedience and protest? Is it morally defensible to appeal to violence when the Christian churches have never been challenged seriously to undertake Jesus' Third Way?

The other likelihood (barring a successful United Nations intervention) is even more horrifying: a guerrilla war fought with inadequate logistical support used by the armed forces of South Africa to justify a genocidal assault on the black population. The black townships are laid out in grids, in most cases well away from the white areas. They could not have been designed more perfectly for obliteration by carpet-bombing. A hot guerrilla war would provide all the warrant needed by military officers chafing at the bit, longing to apply their own version of the "final solution."

But let us suppose that by some remarkable twist of history the military forces of apartheid were to act with uncharacteristic restraint, and allow black insurgents to gain a foothold. A Lebanon-type situation might then result, with decades of low-level warfare wracking the land and neither side able to secure a definitive peace or victory. It is in the very nature of such confrontations that the worst elements in both camps rise to the top—people of uncomplicated power-lust, incapable of seeing anything of God in the enemy and dedicated to their extermination. Even if one side finally did prevail, by then every leader of moderation would have been discredited or assassinated, and the state of the nation would be worse than before.

Perhaps, after protracted struggle, blacks could prevail by violence over white South Africans. We have already noted the fearlessness of black youth, their readiness to die, and their heightened militancy. Observers also point out a new quality of viciousness, a disdain for the advice and control of parents, and a take-no-prisoners mentality among these youth. They would probably not cotton to the moderate, humane policies of a Nelson Mandela, or of any other older black leader who might come to power. Then, South Africa might suffer the fate of Pol Pot's Cambodia, where first enemies, then neutrals, then rival factions, and finally allies and friends were liquidated in a blood bath of horrendous proportions.

Even if that scenario were mercifully averted, and a successful revolution were to be waged, would it not still make sense for the churches to have thrown themselves first into the search for a nonviolent solution? Would it not be better to have exhausted that possibility before large-scale massacres and indiscriminate killing become the order of the day? In short, can anyone cogently argue that the church should not be offering itself to God now as an instrument for fostering a nonviolent struggle for justice in South Africa?

Most of those who provide a theological rationale for revolutionary violence do not appear to be engaged in such violence. Nor, I suspect, do they ever plan to become involved. Historically, people who discuss the necessity of violence seem content to let others be violent on their behalf. Talk of violence may seem to be an indication of increased radicalization, but is it? Most of these Christians have not been engaged previously in militant nonviolent opposition to the government. Their forte has been issuing statements, making pronouncements. Now what are they doing? Engaging in acts of sabotage? Blowing up police stations? Perhaps a few of them are. But most of them are continuing to do what they have done all along: issue statements, make pronouncements, this time about violence. Nothing really has changed.

My gravest anxiety is that this book, rather than actually inciting people to engage in direct acts of nonviolent civil disobedience, will simply be used as an argument against violence. *This book is not an argument against violence.* It is a brief for Jesus' Third Way. I hope at least I have succeeded in making it clear that I would vastly prefer that someone take up violence against the regime than remain passive. Surely the authors of the *Kairos Document* agonized over the same issue. Are people responding to its intention, or are they simply engaged in debating its language?

I suggest that before every discussion of violence and nonviolence, someone should draw a line across the room and invite all who are prepared to give their lives for liberation to step across. Then these, and these only, would be permitted to discuss the question of means.

Rather than see concerned Christians limp between

two opinions, I would urge them to commit themselves fully to militant nonviolence now, at last. (For the churches have never regarded nonviolence as part of the gospel, nor taken the lead in nonviolent training or resistance.) Then, if nonviolence seems to have failed, I would urge them to take up arms and actually fight. We will also need to discuss criteria for judging failure, since after twenty-seven years people still have not concluded that violence has failed either. But to debate the issue interminably, while neither bearing arms nor nonviolently confronting the government, is to play right into the government's hands.

It is true that the apartheid regime continually arrests new leaders who might provide Third-Way leadership. This is not a new problem, and groups of every sort have found ways to continue even with their leadership in jail. Students have been especially adept at building "leaderless" coalitions in which decentralized decision making has enabled them to operate despite the presence of informers and repeated crackdowns by police. And this type of leadership is providing blacks training for the democratic future of the nation.

I freely acknowledge that the apartheid regime is shrewd, and has been extremely effective in divide-and-rule tactics as well as straight repression. Nonviolence is difficult in South Africa, yes, but violence is even more difficult. Twenty-seven years of violence have accomplished very little. Almost all the small victories blacks have won have come through strikes, sitdowns, slowdowns, stayaways, boycotts, rent refusals, funeral demonstrations, symbolic acts and so forth. Nonviolence is virtually the *only* thing that has been working in South Africa.

It is time the churches claim the gospel at its center and throw themselves into nonviolent struggle with a whole heart.

As of October 1987, the emergency decrees in force in South Africa have had the apparent effect of successfully repressing much of the dissent and demonstrations that characterized the two years before they were enacted. It is too early to judge, but it appears that the South African government has, by flexing its muscles, cooled the sense of imminent victory that fired many black youth. Resentment will continue to burst out here and there, but such convulsions of outrage and fear fall far short of a concerted movement for liberation. The churches alone cannot supply the leadership necessary to galvanize opposition into a front of iron resistance, but it can provide several critically needed elements: the destruction of the moral legitimacy of apartheid; the awakening of Christians to the evil of complicity in that system; the moral imperative to offer one's life to God on behalf of justice and truth in society; and, above all, Jesus' Third Way as a means of struggle for the humanization of every party in the conflict.

The Third Way means that those who engage in it do not have to wait for the revolution to succeed before they can begin being fully human. They do not have to let themselves be further dehumanized by hatred and killing. They can begin living the reality of a nonracist society now, and take the consequences. Especially within the fellowship of the churches themselves, they can begin behaving the way the whole society should be behaving. Those churches which are already doing this are losing members and money. But some are also gaining new members, inspired by the sight of a church finally being faithful.

And the loss of certain members can be a blessing, freeing the church to take even greater risks. Clergy will lose their jobs, congregations will split, fulfilling Jesus' prophecy that he did not come to bring peace but division (Luke 12:51). Such is the power of truth that we cannot but love it even when it costs us all that we hold dear.

Perhaps I am being naive, but I believe in the power of God to bring about miracles. So I am praying, and I beg you also to pray, dear readers, for the churches of South Africa, that the miracle will indeed come about: that the churches will wake from their complicity, blindness, and fear, and that, baptized in the fire of nonviolent opposition, they will emerge from that fire purified and regenerated. Let us pray for the liberation of all South Africa's peoples.

More Resources
from New Society Publishers

WRITINGS ON
CIVIL DISOBEDIENCE AND NONVIOLENCE
by Leo Tolstoy
Foreword by George Zabelka
Introduction by David H. Albert

Here in one volume are most of Tolstoy's major writings on conscience and war. Stressing that the process of peace can only begin with the individual's refusal to participate in state-organized killing, Tolstoy's writings are particularly relevant in an age when warfare is sanitized, packaged, and sold to a populace finding it increasingly difficult to respond in an ethically meaningful way. Tolstoy's message is that we must seek ways to end our moral complicity and cooperation with the economic, social, and political processes which could lead us to nuclear war.

410 pages. Annotated bibliography.
Paperback $10.95
Hardcover $29.95

THE POWER OF THE PEOPLE:
ACTIVE NONVIOLENCE IN THE UNITED STATES
Edited by Robert Cooney & Helen Michalowski

The Power of the People is a pictorial encyclopedia of the struggles of U.S. women and men working for peace and justice through nonviolent action. Included are sections on the roots of American nonviolence, the original peace churches, the first secular peace organizations, the women's rights movements, struggles against slavery, the labor movement, conscientious objection, nuclear pacifism, the Civil Rights movement, nonviolent actions against the Vietnam War, ecological struggles, women's peace encampments and more! Biographical sketches include Jane Addams, William Lloyd Garrison, Frederick Douglass, Emma Goldman, Jeannette Rankin, A.J. Muste, Martin Luther King, Jr., Barbara Deming, Dorothy Day and Cesar Chavez. With more than 300 photographs and illustrations, The Power of the People invites us to reclaim our history, placing our current struggles in the context of a noble and empowering tradition.

Large format. 272 pages. Illustrated.
More than 300 photographs. Bibliography. Index.
Paperback $16.95
Hardcover $39.95

SEEDS OF PEACE:
A CATALOGUE OF QUOTATIONS
Compiled and edited by Jeanne Larson & Madge Micheels-Cyrus

Seeds of Peace is an indexed and well-organized collection of more than 1700 quotations on war and peace, nonviolence, and the quest for justice. It includes 29 chapters, including sections on patriotism, waging war, the challenge to make peace, peace conversion, visions of peace, humor, bumper stickers and graffiti, and more. Designed for easy use with tabbed pages, *Seeds of Peace* is a wonderful gift book, as well as an invaluable resource for sermon writers and speechmakers. It's also fun just to browse through!

288 pages. Illustrated. Tabbed pages.
Paperback $12.95
Hardcover $34.95

SPEAKING OF FAITH:
GLOBAL PERSPECTIVES ON WOMEN, RELIGION AND SOCIAL CHANGE
Edited by Diana L. Eck and Devaki Jain
Foreword by Rosemary Radford Ruether

The authors of *Speaking of Faith* include 26 women author/activists from five continents and representing all major religions—including Carol Gilligan, Sisela Bok, Julia Esquivel, Nawal el Saadawi, Radha Bhatt, Judith Plaskow, Beverly Harrison, and Jean Zaru. Speaking from experience, they challenge religious institutions, work toward changing leadership roles, and build a common foundation for social change.
"This book is in itself a model of feminist process and a provocative symbol of global interdependence."
—Annette Huizenga, *Daughters of Sarah*

288 pages.
Paperback $9.95
Hardcover $29.95